"This is a story that reveals what is possible even when you think it's not. It beautifully shows how surrender opens the door to grace. Stephanie Rutt shares depth and insight in all she does."

—AMY LEIGH MERCREE, author of *Aura Alchemy*

"My cup now overflows to receive levels of understanding through this beautifully written book, *Dancing on the Moon*. Stephanie Rutt writes with bare honesty, connecting with your own soul to journey together closer to God like never before. I read this twice without stopping because I didn't want it to end. I realize now that her shared experiences will keep the reader immersed in continued blessings and spiritual growth that will never end."

—TEAL L. GRAY, author of *Shades of Angels*

"Stephanie Rutt may invite us to dance with the moon but, through her collection of vignettes, she invites us to dance with her through the deep heat of the south and the Maine woods of the north, through heritage and legacy, through relationship joys and tears, always keeping step with the Unseen Hand of the Beloved that holds her close in the delight of disguise."

—LAWRENCE JAY, executive director, Rolling Ridge Retreat and Conference Center

"This memoir of spiritual self-discovery through life experiences touched my soul. I sang, cried, and laughed along Stephanie Rutt's journey as if I were there to witness this discovery. Rutt's poignant stories through life offered me confirmation to my spiritual journey, in particular to trust and have faith in the 'Unseen Hand'. I highly recommend this brilliantly written book to anyone on a life of self-discovery."

—RHONDA SCHIENLE, founder, Interfaith Ministry Services

"I have known Stephanie Rutt for fifty-five years. Reading this personal story of her life has touched my heart deeply. Rutt has a brilliant quest for learning and constantly seeks ways to share this knowledge with others. This memoir is a work of true love and appreciation of her roots, devotion to family, unique goodness to cultures, her resilience, her awareness of nature, love of the human spirit, and belief in the goodness of God. Reading her memoir allows you to feel her reality in life but also her deep care about the unknown and the search for answers."

—JANE MASSEY, adjunct professor of education, Mississippi State University

"Stephanie Rutt has been in my life for years, impacting it with laughter and adventure every step of the way. She has always been a beautiful poet, but it shines in her prose during the telling of her stories in her memoir. The writing is musical, and the story is magical. It takes you on a journey of looking at life as an awe-filled series of challenges interspersed with the joy of discovering life where, when choices become infused with love or worry, she always chooses love. Enjoy that love and that journey with my beloved friend."

—SALLY GRUMBLES, speech pathologist

"Stephanie Rutt is a master teacher and mystic, a lover of 'the One to whom I can only point.' In her spiritual memoir, she shares stories of her experiences of this love which has called her to live a non-ordinary life. Rutt's heroine journey through sorrow and joy, pain and passion illuminates for the reader her tender encounters with the divine mystery as she struggles to recover from loss, wrestles with racial injustice, and learns to see the One Love everywhere. Readers will be inspired to recognize moments of their own dance on the moon as they are gently guided by a woman who knows who she is because she knows to whom she belongs."

—CAROL LaCHANCE, author of *The Way of the Mother*

Dancing on the Moon

Dancing on the Moon

The Non-Ordinary Life I Never Saw Coming,
A Spiritual Memoir

STEPHANIE RUTT

Foreword by Albert J. LaChance

RESOURCE *Publications* • Eugene, Oregon

DANCING ON THE MOON
The Non-Ordinary Life I Never Saw Coming, A Spiritual Memoir

Resource Publications
An Imprint of Wipf and Stock Publishers
199 W. 8th Ave., Suite 3
Eugene, OR 97401

www.wipfandstock.com

PAPERBACK ISBN: 979-8-3852-1862-2
HARDCOVER ISBN: 979-8-3852-1863-9
EBOOK ISBN: 979-8-3852-1864-6

08/21/24

To Miss Shirley Curtis, who heard something I could not
and ignited my path.

Contents

Foreword

The book you hold in your hands has been written by a woman who has, through deep spiritual work in many different traditions, restored the innocence of her soul and matured into dignity. Dignity is the state of being that we recognize almost immediately as spiritual authority. Likewise, we are instantaneously aware of our own experience of respect for that dignity. That feeling of deep respect is my signal that this person has, through the power of mysticism, experienced the oneness of all living things.

The oneness of habitat, the biosphere, the presence of the rivers that flow in our veins, the air in our lungs, and the food in our bellies. Through this oneness we become aware of what I call the Phenomenon of the Sacred behind and supporting everything. Each of us is the presence of Divine Dignity and our joy or the lack of it reminds us how well or poorly we serve as the mirrors of God. Stephanie's great longing is to be a reflection of the God she seeks, and the reader will find this truth throughout this book.

The first time I met my teacher, Fr. Thomas Berry, he began his lecture to us with these words: "It's all a question of story." What I came to understand in his words is that the way we experience the story of the universe, earth, all life and culture, as well as how we experience the story of our own life becomes the way we see and hear the creation and indeed the meaning of ourselves. In this book, you will find stories that touch on what it means to journey with God, often by taking the road less traveled, the "non-ordinary life." The path laid out through these stories shows us that the road is the journey. It speaks to us if we listen.

With vulnerability, Stephanie shares how she overcomes personal suffering and rejection through her discovery of her love for the One to whom she belongs. These are stories of the God of surprise, who shows us up in our lives unexpectedly over and over again and speaks through circumstance. There are stories of sorrow, as in her childhood's realization of racial injustice in the South and her inability to change it. There are stories of healing as in "A Blessing from Medjugorje" (p. 92). We learn from the story of how the rosary, a symbol from my own childhood, offers Stephanie the way to discover the healing that Mary bestows. While all Catholics might not agree, for me and for Stephanie, the presence of Mary is a privilege, the presence of the feminine consciousness, the Mother of God.

Rev. Dr. Rutt has studied, taught, counseled, journeyed, and danced in ways that make her the spiritual heroine that she is to many of us. As such, she speaks for us all with the courage to mirror the dignity of our love but also to remind us of the dignity we yearn for and have been denied. She touches on this denial of dignity and shows us a child's confusion at our failure to see beyond the color of someone's skin. She shares the dignity and wisdom of the native peoples, from whom she inherits the art of shamanic journeying. She pays tribute to those suffering from mental, physical, and spiritual pain in every moment of their lives, people we often choose not to see. Reminiscent of Bob Dylan's early musing, she too asks how often do we simply turn our heads and not see? These stories remind us to "see." Stephanie reminds us that we are Homo sapiens, yes, but that our real species call is to be children of God. By restoring our innocence, we come to hear the Voice of God in the innocence of flowers, earth, stars, galaxies, all that lives and dies and lives again . . . Yes, the Voice speaking through creation is the Voice of the Creator. Those with ears to hear hear that Voice, as Stephanie clearly states. Those with eyes to see can see the Creator in all creation.

Stephanie calls us to be ready to drop our frenetic agendas and begin to walk softly on the earth. To be present to the God that is in everyone and everything. She encourages us to fall in love again, to be willing to be innocents in a far from innocent world. When we do, she promises that our lives, our purposes and our many loves will reveal the Voice we long to hear. The call of the human, laughter, will return. Dignity will be restored. We all need an owner's manual on how to live with innocence and dignity. The book in your hands is one such guide. Read with pleasure, find your innocence, and your dignity will follow. We are all lonely and searching, but we are not alone.

Thank you, Stephanie, for finding God and being found by God. Thank you for becoming "a reflection of the One living just beyond my understanding, the One to whom I can only point" (p. xiii).

Thank you for inviting us to the dance.

ALBERT J. LaCHANCE, PhD
Author of numerous books on spirituality, psychology, ecology and religion, including *The Way of Christ: The Gospel of John Through the Unitive Lens* and *The Modern Christian Mystic: Finding the Unitive Presence of God.*

Preface

Funny thing about the moon. It only shines by reflecting the sun's rays. I, too, can take little credit for this non-ordinary life, for any light I've been blessed to shine has certainly come directly from God. Yes, it's true, I've yearned for nothing more than to be a reflection of the One living just beyond my understanding, the One to whom I can only point. But, still, I harbor no illusion it's been me, in any way, who's created all the moments of grace I've known.

And even more wondrously, in the end, I've come to see that those most debilitating circumstances, the insurmountable crippling fear, were a small price to pay for what I've received, as I was made to blossom not *in spite of* but *because of*. And where there'd only been the long night did come the light of day, and, arising from the pit of despair, came love. And where before I could only see the world through my shrouded lens, I came to see the face of God everywhere.

Still, I don't fully understand. Never will. But it's okay. Even better really. It's a mystery, after all, living quite outside the bounds of my loosely threaded thoughts, feelings, and dreams. A mystery hiding in the folds of everyday life and quite fond of revealing itself in unexpected ways. Such times leave me a bit unhinged but also a little freer from the shackles of my inner prisoner. Like snapshots captured in old photographs, they seem to freeze the moment, inviting me to pause and look with soft eyes, to slowly sense the mysterious, the non-ordinary, hiding beyond the faded and crinkled edges.

In these pages, I offer you a few of those snapshots from the non-ordinary life I never saw coming. Perhaps by pausing by each one you'll recognize something of yourself, delight in a new possibility or, simply, tuck something away to revisit at a later time. Mostly, my hope is that you'll discover, beyond the faded details, a place where, though strangers, we meet and know one another.

Acknowledgments

This memoir came into form largely due to the expert guidance of my editor, Alice Peck of Alice Peck Editorial. For two years, Alice led me from the big picture design to discovering how all the pieces could fit together. Along the way, she suggested, reflected, supported, and, most of all, brought her full presence to me and my work. It was a gift beyond measure.

I also want to thank all of those who agreed to read the initial draft and offer an endorsement. Your support in this way, especially at the beginning, was so very encouraging. Each of you, too, brought a special gift to this memoir.

I want to offer a most special thank you to Dr. Albert J. La-Chance for writing such a beautiful foreword, perfectly complementing this work. Albert took the time to synchronize his heart and thoughts to my words in such a meaningful way. I will be forever grateful for his spirit, long walk with the Sacred, and for our spiritual kinship. I'd also like to thank his wife, Rev. Carol La-Chance, former Director of the Tree of Life Interfaith Seminary, for reading and offering her thoughtful reflections.

Finally, I'd like to thank my husband, Doug, who's always been my most ardent supporter, who's read every draft of every book, blog, and article I've ever published. Mostly, his continued encouragement to tell my story has been the biggest blessing.

And, most of all, to the One who made me and this recording of my non-ordinary life possible. It, and I, belong to You.

Introduction

When the Katydids Went Silent

It felt like a sucker punch, lightning quick, freezing me in the moment. Not from the one I loved the most. Not from the one who'd called me Baby for as long as I could remember and even had a picture of me in his wallet, the one taken when I was three years old out in the front yard, giggling, trying hard to stand still. Being Easter, I had on a brand-new white dress with a red sash and a big bow right in front. No, not from the one who'd taken me "over town" for drippy ice cream cones on hot summer days. I'd stand in the middle of the front seat of the old forty-nine Ford until I got too tall and my head hit the roof. Not from the one who'd make a big pot of oatmeal each morning singing, "Oh, Danny boy, the pipes, the pipes are calling . . ." And certainly not from the one who'd read to me every night from the *Reader's Digest*, though I had no idea what the stories meant. Didn't matter. This was my special time with my granddaddy—the one I'd counted down the months, weeks, and then, finally, the days until it was time to go see him again each summer. There was also my grandmother, Nanny, but in those early years she was fully eclipsed by my granddaddy. It wasn't until his passing when I was sixteen that I discovered her, and over the years we, too, would become very close.

During the school year I lived alone with my mom, an elementary school teacher, in another part of the country. Sadly, consumed with her own deep disappointments, sorrow, and anger, she could barely hold herself up, much less me. Struggling under the crushing unfairness that seemed to have already deadened her young life, she simply couldn't gather me in. My father had left before I was born—not a good scenario for a young single mother in 1950 in the Deep South. I was grown before I would meet him, and my two half-siblings, and would only see him a few more times in later years.

But as a child, just knowing summer would finally come around again and we'd be packing up to make the long drive back home, as we called it, to my grandparents' house, could make the Good Fairy appear to fill in all the empty corners of my lonely days with her magical dust. It was magical because those few short weeks each summer were like Christmas, my birthday, and every other holiday rolled into one, as then, and only then, I'd become someone's baby, and that someone even had a picture of me in his wallet.

I'd turned ten that summer of the sucker punch; my body was changing. But my new budding was the farthest thing from my mind when I could finally see the old county road winding toward the fork ahead. A right turn meant I'd get to see my grandparents' farmhouse beyond the pasture where the cows grazed. I loved the cows.

When, at last, the supper dishes were done and the sounds of the katydids and tree frogs filled the air, I knew it'd soon be time for bed, so I rushed in to crawl up beside him leaning back against the rusty, iron, curved headboard as I'd always done. He, as usual, was reading the *Reader's Digest*, and I, feeling like a kid on one of those long-awaited Christmas mornings, couldn't wait for the story to begin.

But, instead . . . silence.

And then, "Go on now. Go on. You're too old," he said with a quick glance at me—a glance I'd later remember as being one of clear finality yet also tinged with just a hint of regret, maybe sadness, or both.

I couldn't move.

"Go on now," but this time he kept staring at the page.

Somehow, I pulled myself off the bed and started walking toward the door. About halfway, I stopped and looked back. He hadn't moved. I stood frozen, caught, snagged—like when an un-suspecting animal feels the steel trap crashing down. Desperately I wanted to rewind to when I'd leaped up next to him, giddy and free. But couldn't. And I wanted to run away. But couldn't. All I could do was stand there, now in a silent void, staring blankly at nothing, barely noticing the tears coming until I could taste them on my lips.

"Go on now. Go on." He never looked up.

I don't remember the rest of that summer. What I do remember was when we returned home, I started to stutter. School, in particular, was unbearable. Filmstrip days were the worst, and it seemed we had a lot of them. When I'd first hear the sound of the projector coming, those metal wheels grating on the concrete outside, I'd start to feel my insides darting frantically back and forth, as that old feeling of being snagged and trapped would come over me. Then, one by one, as we each read aloud, and my turn got closer and closer, I'd feel that steel trap snap, locking me down. No escape, freezing me, and then sheer panic would set in. Sometimes, some of the kids would already be pointing at me, snickering, jeering, feeding a frenzy that would soon culminate in the much-anticipated main event—watching my contorted face cringe, trying hard, so hard, to push, push out each trapped sound. And me . . . all I could do was laugh right along with them.

As I grew older, I gradually found ways to hide my stutter: changing a word mid-sentence, cleverly skipping over words that started with certain letters and, most especially, avoiding, at all cost, situations where I'd have to say my name. Then one day, when I was a sophomore in high school, my world was altered in a way I couldn't have imagined—a sentiment I'd find myself saying many times over in my life.

It happened at the end of a public speaking class, required of course, or I'd certainly never have been there! I'd read a story I'd written with minimal stuttering, and, afterwards, the teacher, Miss Shirley Curtis, to whom this memoir is dedicated and whose face I can remember in every detail, asked me to stay after class. She told me, in quite a matter-of-fact way, she was going to recommend me for what was then called the school forensics club, which included the debate team and was responsible for sponsoring speech tournaments, because she said, "You have something to say."

Now clearly, I couldn't hold such a thing so, as soon as school was out, I rushed home, shaking, trying hard to hold down the nauseous curdling about to erupt out of me. The thought of getting up in front of people to give speeches—well, felt like I'd be stepping off into some dark abyss to a certain death—only that would have been preferable. But my voice, a voice that had any possibility of speaking, to make my own decisions about things, was silent, nowhere to be found. So, I complied.

Oh, but little did I know what was coming. About that time, my mom and I had started going to a new church called the First Church of Religious Science founded on the teachings of *The Science of Mind* by Earnest Holmes. It planted the interfaith seed in my heart but, more importantly at that time, was teaching me something about prayer. So, knowing there was absolutely *no* way I could ever do any of those speeches on my own, as I sat there in agony waiting for my name to be called, I'd be praying hard: "P-l-e-a-s-e God, speak for me because I can't do it. I just can't."

And, each time, feeling like I was stepping off into that dark abyss, to my most unexpected would-have-never-believed-it surprise, instead of death I found a kind of soft landing in the hand of God—the only way I've ever been able to describe it. And me, I'd be standing there listening and sometimes just marveling at what God was having me say and how eloquently he was having me say it.

Though I didn't have the words for it at the time, being forced to step off into that abyss required nothing short of complete and total surrender—no faking this one—yet, as each time I'd find myself, so graciously, landing in that soft hand, I quickly began to trust it much more than I'd ever think to trust myself. For reasons I couldn't possibly fathom or explain, I had the most intimate loving friend walking with me every step of the way—a friend who'd always speak for me when I could not and save me from that terrifying abyss. And, little by little, I started to know a kind of joy—not the kind that comes and goes but is steady and solid, quiet and still, living deep under the outer trembling of my life. And it let me know, again and again, I'd be okay.

And a love started growing inside me. Bigger than me. Spilling out. The first time was at our church camp at Asilomar, California. I was standing in a large circle singing our closing song on the last day, "Let There be Peace on Earth." Quite unexpectedly, I knew, *knew*, without any doubt, I was one with every person in that circle—that the God in me was the very same in them—and we were all one. And I started to cry tears I'd never felt before, softly convulsing from some inner waking ecstasy to which I could only point but never describe.

When I got home, it continued. I could *see* God now behind the sorrowful eyes of the cashier at the counter. Beyond the glance of the one begging for change. Hidden in the heart of the stranger passing by. And, over the years, God continued to find me again and again, appearing in unsuspecting ways as he steadily sculpted this non-ordinary life I never saw coming: branding me early on, crumbling life as I knew it, preparing me for the life waiting; startling me with his voice; purging my deepest wounds; and, using me to heal my family's secrets and shame. He sent me on a journey to discover him moving me into stillness; to hear him in the silent echoes of my prayers; and to find him peering at me from beyond the veil. He frolicked with me in the sweet valleys and laid me on the altar of death atop the summit covered only with grace. He confronted me on sidewalks, drive-through windows, from behind prison walls, and sent me to play with the little ones, fairies in disguise. And he birthed me wild and free in nature's hidden places. Coming full circle, he directed me to give back all I'd received and, finally, left me with only a picture in my pocket before propelling me into the fire to claim me fully as his own.

Now, there is nowhere God is not.

And I know now that the stutter early on was the essential beginning, necessary to lay me bare, with nothing left but the silent scream of my prayer. Still, if I know anything for certain, it's that I could never have had the non-ordinary life I've had had it not been for that stutter, something I absolutely *knew* I could never overcome on my own. And, even at this writing, I can still hardly find the breath, the words, to say, "Thank you." No, it feels like the words just fall short into a bottomless sky. After all, what can possibly be said when you've been given the world, life, and been made to shine like moonlight?

Throughout adulthood my struggle to speak has essentially healed. Still, I hold the memory of those early years, tender and protected. A memory that continues to compel me to ask my God to speak for me before I need to talk publicly in any way. It's for this reason I only use dot points or a brief outline. I *never* write anything out. I prepare my list and then let God have the floor. It frees me and, as it's always been, I'm just so amazed to witness what God can do.

I know there'll be many who'll be surprised to read my story: those who perhaps met me in later years; those who've only known me in professional or academic settings; even some who may have known me growing up in the summers at my grandparents', for it remained the only place and time I felt carefree and relaxed. And when you've been blessed, as I have, by so many moments of grace, I suspect there'll be naysayers. It's okay. I don't write for them. I write for all those who struggle with something and hope for relief that never seems to come. I write to give hope, share inspiration, and offer possibility.

I'm fond of saying I'm so glad I'm not in charge of my life because, left to my own devices and understandings, I could've never imagined it unfolding as it has. I could've never discovered the limitless joy, wonder and freedom that comes when my soul is completely disarmed and surrendered, pulsing with nothing but divine curiosity. But I'll let you be the judge as you read the stories here. Remember, I'm no different from you as I'm not a celebrity and my story, on the surface, isn't particularly unique. After all, we all have something. Yet, oddly, it's *because* of this I'm hoping you'll find yourself in my stories and discover things there to serve your journey.

Who knows? Maybe you, too, will find yourself dancing on the moon.

The journey home takes you off the known way.

Follow.

When thunder claps and chilly rain whips your face

Find your pulse . . .
the One who beats your heart.

Feel the rise and fall of your chest . . .
the One who breathes you.

Rise up bold . . . barefoot
and enter through Love's narrow gate

onto the field of wonder.

PART 1

Awakening

1

Jarred Awake

Hidden Pearls

When the cool earth beneath your feet
becomes brittle with sharp rocks . . .

When the way
becomes steep and feels insurmountable . . .

Scream.
And change shoes.

The Scar

Not long after being sent out to compete in speech tournaments, something happened leaving my face permanently scarred—a branding—only in the best way possible.

"You'll be fine," the nurse said. "What a blessing you were asleep."

I didn't know what'd happened. I just knew no one would give me a mirror to see why blood kept coming into my eyes, and they wouldn't let me sit up. I was drifting in and out of consciousness in a small emergency room, the closest to where, I would later learn, the accident had happened. I was sixteen.

We were on our way home from a Religious Science church camp. Most of our youth group had ridden in a van to and from, but two of us were able to ride in the car with our group leaders, Mr. and Mrs. Franklin. My friend Sally and I had volunteered to ride home with them.

We were all giggly and happy coming off several days of camp as we rode along a lonely stretch of highway in the foothills. I have no memory of seeing the other car, feeling us swerve, or the impact. One moment I was awake, goofing off with Sally, and the next I was trying to blink away blood dripping down my face. I was squeezed in tight behind Mr. Franklin in the driver's seat, my back pressed against the door, facing the inside of the car. Mr. Franklin was trying to talk, trying to find out if we were okay. Sally was awake but had deep cuts on her face and some of her teeth had been knocked out. Her mouth was bleeding. Mrs. Franklin was slumped over, right in front of me, not moving. *Why isn't she moving?* Unfortunately, it took quite a while for help to come as we were far away from the nearest town.

After days in intensive care, an extended stay in the hospital, and an initial operation to close up the hole between my eyes, I started to piece together the full breadth of what had happened. A young man had been out in the foothills and had pulled back onto the road as we came around a bend. Thankfully, Mr. Franklin had only sustained minor injuries, but, tragically, Mrs. Franklin had been killed on impact. Both men in the other car had also suffered serious injuries. It was thought I must have been thrown around and, at some point, hit the door lock knob to finally land behind Mr. Franklin. This was, of course, long before seatbelts.

When I returned to school, I felt terribly self-conscious. I just so wanted to hide. My face was dented in, the space between my eyes was flat, and only a part of my nose remained. Sometimes I'd put a band-aid over what used to be my bridge to try and hide it somehow. It was a very long year before I'd have another surgery to build back my bridge and have a piece of bone tissue inserted to lengthen my nose. But things hadn't gone as planned, so to this day I have a dent between my eyes. What I couldn't have known was the so-called botched surgery, as some described it, became a key part of God's plan.

"You'll be fine. What a blessing you were asleep." Several doctors would say the same. I don't remember when I first began to realize the enormity of the blessing this simple statement held. How could I have been fully awake and happy one moment and then, in the next, not? Slowly, I began to know that, surely, some kind of intervention had occurred on my behalf that day. This would be my first introduction to the mystery beyond my struggle to speak, the first of many times I'd fully know that God's unseen hand was in charge of my life.

And how was being left with a scar a key part of the plan? Still today, when I look in the mirror, sometimes I'll pause and quietly remember the One who, I believe, put me to sleep that day . . . that divine anesthesiologist passing his unseen hand over my face.

And I remember, without a doubt, to whom it is I belong.

Freed

A little over a decade later, another totally unforeseen incident would irrevocably end life as I'd known it and would open the way for the life I was destined to have—that life I never saw coming.

It all started in a whirlwind. I was in my first year of teaching at a middle school in Pensacola, Florida. One night, a couple of the other single teachers and I went to a dance being held at the Officer's Club at the Naval Base. And like a movie script being played out in slow motion, there he was, and I thought he was the most gorgeous thing I'd ever seen. We started dating, but three months later he got orders for Yuma, Arizona, so we got engaged and I started planning our spring wedding. We'd never even had a disagreement, much less a real argument. Such was the wisdom of my twenty-three years.

Very soon after our marriage, the impact of the mistake we'd made was on full display. By then, we were living in Kaneohe, Hawaii, but even the lure of such an exciting place couldn't keep our unhappiness at bay. I, in particular, having absolutely no familiarity with military life, found myself constantly at odds with just about every commonly accepted practice. Something as simple as going to the movies:

"Why can't we sit in the balcony?"

"That's for enlisted personnel," Dean would say.

"So?" I'd complain.

And I felt least at home with the other officers' wives. I didn't play bridge or enjoy social drinking in the middle of the day and was even less interested in finding my place in the pecking order of the club.

Instead, I found a small Samoan community on a lovely stretch of beach and set up my table right next to them making and selling puka shell jewelry. Over time, I became close to one couple, Ilene and Failla, and, at least on the beach, we enjoyed a nice camaraderie. But no, this was not considered acceptable behavior for a young officer's wife whose primary job was to support the optimum advancement of her husband's career. But it *was* who I was, and joining the Samoans, in some ways, foreshadowed a lifelong tendency to leave the more established pathways to forge my own. Still, my discontent with military life must have been very disappointing, challenging, and frustrating for Dean in ways I couldn't see or appreciate at the time.

When we returned to the States, I was pregnant with our first child, and it felt destiny had set in. I was a good girl (emphasis on "good," and I use the word "girl" purposefully), and Dean was from a conservative Greek family. Any previous thoughts of perhaps walking away from our unhappiness were now silently relegated to the place of old dreams.

I dove into being a traditional wife and mother, though I had no model for such a thing. I learned how to make excellent Greek dishes and how to throw a great dinner party or neighborhood cookout. I made special wall hanging rugs and handmaid Christmas stockings and always had homemade birthday cakes. And delightfully, I discovered I loved those parts of my life, as it felt like I was creating for my family what I'd so missed as a child. Yet, underneath it all, there was always this lingering hope that just maybe, if I tried hard enough, made it all perfect enough, the dull pain between Dean and me would go away. It didn't. Two years later, our second child was born, six months before the incident, irrevocably ending life as I'd known it.

It was a Friday night, and I'd finished up the dishes and gotten our girls to bed. Dean was sitting in the rocking chair in the living room, which I thought was odd, as he'd always sat in the den to watch TV. I don't remember even sitting down before he said, "I don't love you anymore. I'm leaving for a while." I stood stunned, unable to move. And, before I could grasp what was happening, he'd gotten up and walked out.

I was sure he'd call or return the next day. He didn't. Not the next day, or the next. When well over a week had passed with no word, I called my best friend, Jane, who lived about four hours away. She packed up her six-month-old baby and came to stay with me for a week. That time literally saved me, as my usual inner fortitude was quickly crumbling.

The day before she'd arrived, I'd gone to the grocery store. Some song had come on over the store speaker that had landed the final blow to my already unsteady footing. I ran out to the car, leaving the cart filled, and then got lost. I found myself on the side of a road I didn't recognize, crying uncontrollably and feeling truly afraid I wasn't going to find my way home.

Jane has often said it felt like someone had died when she stayed with me. She was right. It was me—or the me then. Yet, absolutely no one could have told me that, in fact, a great blessing was being played out—one that would truly change the course of my life.

Over the coming weeks, I started to regain my footing enough to begin to stand a little stronger in myself. So on the day when Dean finally did come home, expressing deep regret, the girl he'd left standing there seemed to have, in some ways, faded and in her place, barely emerging, was someone new—a woman—and this woman didn't want to go back. She didn't want to settle for the inevitable unhappiness. It was like his walking out had broken some kind of spell. The contract was now null and void. I had absolutely no idea how I was going to make it on my own. I just knew I didn't want how it'd always been. We divorced a year later. Dean left for an overseas deployment and I found a job.

Being a single mom started the hardest few years that to this day leave me with deep compassion for all moms who have to go it alone. Though I had great friends and neighbors, my nearest relative was an aunt over an hour away. She tried to be as supportive as possible, but I was alone for the two a.m. fevers, nighttime dinners, baths, and stories after an exhausting day at work. There was no one else to wake early to make and pack the lunch boxes and get my girls dressed to go. And no one else to make sure I got to the daycare on time to pick them up before the late fees kicked in.

Most challenging was when one or all of us were sick. One time I remember in particular: I'd started having a throbbing sore throat during the day and, when I picked up my girls, they too were sniffly and cranky. On the way home both started crying and one had a full-blown accident, diarrhea, all over the car seat and the back seat. After getting us in and changing clothes, I put on a can of soup I thought would help us all feel a little better until I could get dinner ready.

By this time, I could hardly swallow. I was holding my youngest daughter on my hip and my other daughter was clinging to my legs and both were crying really hard—that "make-it-better-right-now!" cry. As I stood there stirring the soup, I was doing all I could not to collapse and cry right along with them. I knew there was still dinner to fix, baths, and, hopefully, a quiet bedtime story before bed. And then there was the car seat and car to clean up before I could crash.

My two beautiful girls were *the* bright spots in my whole fractured life, yet I always felt I was barely present to them as I was trying so desperately to hold myself, our life, together. We did have our fun times, though: rides on my bike around the neighborhood, playing with the hose and kiddy pool in the back yard, going to the park on the weekends and, most special of all, the occasional outing for a kid's meal of hamburgers and fries.

A great blessing being played out. In the years since, I've often said that Dean leaving me was, indeed, the greatest gift because I would've never had the courage to leave him. Wasn't going to happen. Remember the emphasis on "good"? Yes, I was the good one, more prone to accepting unhappiness than disappointing our two families or even to imagine claiming any sense of autonomy of my own. No, I got lucky. I got left—better yet, freed. And, as a result, the girl who'd tried to accept her life withered away, and in her place the woman I would become was born.

One day, when Dean was home on leave and had stopped by to spend some time with our girls, there was a quiet moment between us just as he was getting ready to leave. For one who'd always found it very difficult to express his emotions when we were married, I was caught off guard when he said, "I always knew you wanted something I didn't know how to give you." And his eyes were saying, "I'm sorry." For a few moments we stood there looking at each other, holding each other, in a way it seemed we'd never been able to before. It was affirming and heartbreaking.

From the man of few words, whose comfort zone had always been silence, had come a short sentence that'd said it all . . . and it'd set us both free to move on. And for me, over time, I came to realize that, while I had a right to yearn for the kind of marriage, life, I wanted, I didn't have the right to ask him to be who he was not. There are no victims really. We had each played our part in bringing our lives to that fateful Friday night. And, in the end, it'd be me who'd sever the tie.

Several years later I married Doug, the man who, for me, would show me what real love was all about. Doug also had two great sons I'd come to call my own. Dean too found happiness. He married again and had several more children. Still, over the years, we all came to realize how differently divorce impacts the adults from the children. Adults move on to new relationships. For the children, though, there's no divorce from the mom or dad no longer living with them. No matter how much effort is extended to maintain the bond or how much they may care for the stepparents, one foot may always hold back, rooted deep in a slowly fading dream of what was.

Doug and I have always worked hard to include and hold all parts of our blended and extended family. It's not easy. It's often messy, challenging and complicated. But sweetly, it's also opened our hearts to include more children, and later, in-laws and grand-children to love.

We've been together over forty years now, and I can still look across the room at him and find myself smiling *that* smile . . . some of you ladies will know what I mean . . . the secret one—even an old woman smiles in those private moments of remembering. And we *are* old now, and how strange it is to still feel thirty-something inside yet to see our greying hair and wrinkling skin. No matter. Sometimes his smile, from back across the room, will cause my heart to pause for just a moment, holding all we've known, and I find myself wishing for one more day please, one more day.

Yes, what I once felt was the absolute worst thing that could possibly happen turned out to be the blessing needed to set me free and to discover a man who would gift me in untold ways and a life that would, graciously, support me to become me, and as a result, have that non-ordinary life I never saw coming.

2

Direct Contact

Spirit Flights, Voices, and Angels

Giggle.

You seized my fledging spirit
pierced my stagnant mind
and sat close

Some would call You my imaginary friend . . .

I call You my Love.

Early on, my spiritual journey propelled me into places I'd never imagined, awakening me to what was possible while purging me of long held tears. I was left aching for more . . . but for what, I couldn't say.

Flight

It happened before I had any exposure to shamanism or the practices of indigenous peoples. It was before Doug had seen a necklace hanging on the wall of a Native American crafts store, which he brought home, saying, "This called to me off the wall for you," definitely *not* something I could've imagined him saying at that time. The necklace had an eagle's head carved out of the tip of a deer antler that hung on a black string. It remains one of my most treasured objects.

I was sitting in a circle at Antioch New England Graduate School, a student in the Dance Movement Therapy Program. A visiting teacher had come to lead our class and, after a dance segment, was guiding us in a group meditation. Sometime after she started, I felt my spirit leave my body, go down two flights of stairs, and take to the sky. I'd been missing my grandmother terribly, and somehow knew I was on my way down south to see her. We'd become very close since the passing of my granddaddy.

Soon I found myself inside an eagle spirit, looking out his eyes, as he carried us along. When we arrived at my grandmother's house, I easily separated from him and could feel, quite viscerally, the stone path under my feet that led up to the front porch. As I neared the door, I could hear my grandmother and my aunt talking and could smell the sweet fragrances coming from the kitchen.

Salt pork seasoning the butterbeans. Looked like leftover fried chicken. Sliced tomatoes. Homemade biscuits. They were talking about what to do with one of the trees out front that had taken a hit during a recent rain storm. It looked to be in danger of falling over on the house.

I lingered for a short while and then, feeling satisfied, found myself back inside the eagle spirit again, traveling up north to rejoin my circle at school. As we neared, I separated from the eagle and flew up the two flights of stairs and rested in my body as the guided meditation was ending. We were then each asked to share about our dance and meditation experience.

Now, given that I was completely taken aback, to say the least, and feeling quite shaken by what had happened, I decided I'd remain quiet about it. I needed time to process it all and to find a place to put it that could, maybe, make some kind of sense to me.

Then, "Stephanie, would you like to share now?"

And I heard myself say, "Well, I don't really know what hap . . ."

"I do!" blurted the woman next to me. "You left just after we started and you came back right before we ended." She went on to say how she'd had a similar experience in a group studying with a Peruvian shaman. I couldn't speak. But it felt like an important confirmation of what had happened.

When I got home, I called my grandmother and, being careful not to inadvertently plant suggestions or guide the conversation, I simply wove in at one point, "So, what'd y'all have for dinner today? I sure miss that good southern cookin'."

"Oh, not much. Some fried chicken we brought home from the supper last night, butterbeans, and sliced tomatoes. We've got so many tomatoes I'm gonna have to give some away. And Mae made some biscuits. Not too much."

"Sound great to me," I said. "So, what else's been going on?"

"Oh, we've got to find someone to come and cut down a tree out front—the big one on the other side of the drive. We think it got hit in the storm last week, and now it's leaning over towards the house. It's always something."

In the years since this unexpected flight, with all of my practicing of indigenous spiritual practices, I've never had another experience quite like this one. What I do know is that it's entirely possible to bilocate—to be in two places at one time. But, once again, it happened not of my will but solely of the will of that unseen hand, in this context, known as the Great Spirit. And, somehow, I know if and when it's time for me to use this ability for some greater good, it'll come to me again. Such is the way of the mystery beyond all understanding.

Meanwhile, I continue to practice and honor some of the great teachings from Native American medicine men and women and indigenous peoples around the world. It is a blessing to learn from those who've long held the ancient wisdom of the earth and knowledge of the other realms.

The Voice

The first time I heard an actual voice coming from the other realms—not a deep intuition but an actual voice—was, once again, in a circle at Antioch New England Graduate School. Now some may think that hearing such a voice would be the ultimate insider gift. For me, while it certainly was, and still remains, a unique blessing, the experience now sits quite comfortably among so many other sweet gifts I've received along the way.

It was our normal gathering to start the day. Over time, we'd gotten used to sitting in the same place in our circle but, on this morning, the spot next to me was open, as the woman who usually sat there was late. We all thought this was odd, as she was one who was always early or on time. Suddenly, right before we were to begin, a young girl from across our circle, someone I didn't know very well, got up and came over to sit in the open space next to me and then immediately went into the yoga position known as child's pose. She got on her knees, sat back on her heels, and then leaned forward to put her forehead on the floor. *What in the world is she doing?*

Then I heard, "Put your hand on her back." Startled, I tried to remain calm as I quickly looked around to see if anyone else had heard the voice. No one gave any sign. So, slowly, and as discretely as possible, I put my hand on her back and left it there for about a minute. When I removed my hand, she sat up and said, "Thank you for your healing touch." Then, she went back to her usual place in our circle and the woman who normally sat next to me came in.

For many years, I didn't share this story with anyone aside from Doug and a close friend. At that time, knowing something about abnormal psychology, I was a bit worried about having heard an actual voice. Yet, it had all seemed well, okay, in a way I wasn't quite ready to admit to myself.

That is until the next time . . .

It was a few years later and I was teaching a class in child development at the University of New Hampshire at Manchester. On that particular day, I was lecturing on Piaget's theory of cognitive development. While certainly knowledgeable of the theory, the topic didn't hold a lot of interest for me. More importantly, I wasn't feeling well. Normally, I enjoyed teaching and always looked forward to it, but on this day, I would've much rather stayed home.

My lecture began as usual, but about a third of the way in the connection I'd always enjoyed with that unseen hand, the one I'd always known would speak for me when I could not, suddenly felt unplugged. Gone dead—or so I thought. And, to my horror, I found myself standing there alone—like when I was ten years old. My heart started to race, and I could feel the sheer terror growing inside of me. Anyone who's had a panic attack will know exactly what I'm talking about. I sensed my lips moving but could barely hear the words. Blood was draining from my face. I was going down a rabbit hole fast.

Then, the voice said in a clear, neutral tone, "Keep talking." And once more, "Keep talking."

And I heard myself say, "I'm sorry. I don't feel well. I need to step out for a moment." And I did. After a short break, I rejoined the class and completed the lecture with no effort or concern. I was reconnected and I was good.

In hindsight, I'd remember the neutral voice, completely void of emotion or persuasion, as simply being stone solid. There. With me. It'd been me, personally consumed with resistance, who'd, inadvertently, forgotten to whom it was I belonged. It was I who'd unplugged.

God had been there all along.

The Piano Bench

I still wonder if he was real. In a way, it doesn't matter. It was the gift he gave me—his face with that soft, barely smiling gaze, though he never looked at me directly, and the kindness, close enough to fill my swiftly draining heart as it convulsed with tears.

He and I were only two of three passengers on one of those small puddle-jumper flights from Meridian, Mississippi, to Memphis. He was already on the plane when I and another passenger boarded. The other passenger sat up front, and I sat across from the man. Our puddle-jumper was one of several lined up that day, ready to take travelers to larger cities.

Moments before, I'd been in the hangar waiting for my flight to be called. I was there with my mom and stepfather. My mom had had a stroke a few years before and was in a wheelchair. It was there, in the middle of that cramped, dingy, noisy room filled with strangers, that she looked up at me with *that* look, the one I'd seen a lot, especially since the stroke. The one that seemed to eagerly hone upward as if searching for something—a something that always eluded, something out of sight, beyond reach, a something that could, maybe, somehow dispel, resolve, mend what couldn't quite be named. And, as so many times before, it was just the two of us there, locked in a vortex of memory.

A vortex that held how she'd never regained her footing after my father left. How she'd always worked so hard to hold it all together, but often the weight of sorrow had just been too much to bear, too much to carry.

So, I knew that look. Only lately, it'd made me feel oddly squeamish and unarmed. Now, it was bulldozing right through my strongest yeah buts, right through my best lines and rightful defense. Now it made me anxious and always in a hurry to leave. Little did I know that my heart was about to undergo a final ripping away of all the stiches that had long held it together. And that it would happen when I least expected it—during that final it's-time-to-go hug.

"Okay, mom. Gotta go. Take care of yourself. I love you," I said, bending down to hug her. But it was in the middle of that hug that I felt the first rising of the tsunami swelling in my belly. Like being poked and jarred awake from a dreamy sleep, I suddenly knew, without any doubt, that *I was never going to get what I needed—not because she was bad or cruel—but because she didn't have it. She hadn't gotten it either. She was still looking for it like I was.* It all happened in a second—a second that changed everything.

And as I walked out to the plane, I could feel the tsunami building. When I settled into my seat across from the man, it broke through. Now throttled sounds were surging out of me like a torrent I couldn't control. After years of therapies and healing, it felt like the final, most deeply rooted, vestiges of moldy sorrow and rage were now scouring against my insides, pushing up and out, unabated, toward freedom. Finally, it was all coming undone.

"I'll wave to them for you," he said as he gently tapped the arm of my seat.

I couldn't answer and barely noticed the gesture but at one point did manage to glance at him. He was looking straight ahead, though it seemed his soft gaze was staring at nothing. Much later, I would wonder, with so many people outside to send off the puddle-jumpers, and because he was already on the plane, he couldn't have seen me with my mom and stepdad inside . . . how could he have known who "them" was?

The flight was short, maybe twenty minutes, and by the time we'd landed in Memphis, I was just beginning to regain some composure. When we'd come to a stop, the passenger in the front was first to deplane down the stairs. Then the man next to me got up. As I watched him walk the few steps to the front, I felt compelled to catch up and say, "Thank you" or something to acknowledge the kindness he'd offered from those few inches across the aisle.

As he turned to make his way down the stairs, I put my compact in my purse and got up to follow. The flight attendant and pilot stood at the exit looking at me with polite sympathy—the kind you offer strangers when you want them to know you care but don't want to get too close. I paused and glanced out across the long walkway leading to the terminal. The first passenger was about halfway there. But the man who'd been seated across from me was nowhere in sight.

Now jilted with sudden anxiety, I asked the flight attendant and pilot, "Do you know where the man is . . . the one who was sitting right across from me?" But my voice was already trailing off as I could see that now there was a new sense of concern growing mixed in with that polite sympathy. "There was only you and the man ahead there on the plane, Miss."

For a long time, I was caught up in the mystery of it all. It seemed pretty special to have been visited by an angel or some ethereal being. But as the years wore on, I noticed something different happening—even more special—when I was with my mom. I felt a growing sense of peace around her, a quiet compassion for that deep sorrow I could now see on her face. It also seemed to have something to do with how my own daughters were now grown and how I could, even before I knew it, find myself looking at them with my own version of *that* look.

Something my mom could do that always amazed me was she could play the piano though she'd never been taught. She was one who could hear a song once and play it, full chords and all. One day, shortly before she died, she was playing some of the old hymns, and I did something I'd never done. I gently nudged her over so I could sit close on the piano bench and I started singing the words to some of the hymns. And it was somewhere in the middle of "In the Sweet By and By" that I knew the look had relaxed and the search had ended, if only for a short while, for both of us.

I'm still grateful for the mystery man on the plane, for his kindness and for his tender accompaniment that day when the tsunami had its way with me. But I'm no longer enamored with the notion of visiting ethereal beings. Rather, sometimes I imagine me and my daughters squeezed in close on an old piano bench, singing out full bore some ole catchy tunes and smiling like crazy . . . and, well, that's quite enough heaven for me.

PART II

Dusty Roads

3

A Right at the Fork

Deep Roots

I saw You looking at me
from those eyes faded and worn

And I heard You loud and clear in that voice that couldn't end.

I felt You singing me into the night making all the world silent . . .
even the tree frogs

Like fireflies out late in the yard, You danced . . .
And I was caught.
(lucky me)

I love those small country towns now largely abandoned because, just behind my closed eyes, images play revealing a lost time of vibrancy—a time and place where I began and will forever call home. A place where none of the spiritual names I've acquired over the years from various faith traditions apply. No. Here folks simply say, "That's Mrs. Bishop's grandbaby, you know, Dorothy's daughter." Nothing else need be said. Here, Stephanie is the only spiritual name I need.

The Cedar Chest

I was over forty when I found out about Joe. I was rummaging through my grandmother's cedar chest as I'd done so often in the past during my summer visits. All the old pictures were there, mostly of those taken *down home* where my grandmother had grown up. Among the yellowed and torn pictures were the familiar faces of those I'd long known, mixed in with others I didn't recognize. One such picture was of a teenage boy standing alone out in the yard.

I'd run across this picture before, but this time the face staring back at me held my attention and roused my curiosity. I walked into the kitchen where my grandmother was busy cleaning, moving pots and pans from the stove to the sink.

"Nanny, who's this?"

She looked at the picture briefly and then said matter-of-factly, "That's Joe," as she continued moving the pots and pans. When no further explanation came, I said, "Who's Joe?"

My grandmother never stopped her work nor did she look at me as she offered her brief explanation. "Joe was my younger brother. But he was never right." It was clear to me she was not about to be drawn into any conversation about it. I stood feet glued to the worn, linoleum floor. *What?!* my heart yelled out in a silent cry—a cry I knew was bouncing off the kitchen walls.

It was completely incomprehensible to me that there'd been a family member I'd not known about. I was the one who'd created the family photo albums, wandered through graveyards with my grandmother gathering information about births and deaths, and had started researching our family tree. Then, at one point, I remembered an old family Bible in which my great-grandmother had placed a sheet of paper listing the names and birth dates of her children. The bottom of the sheet had been torn off, but there remained what looked like the top part of the capital letter *O* where the last name would have been added. I'd never paid much attention to the mark before. Now I knew it was the top part of the letter *J*, written in cursive, as the other names had been.

My great-grandmother was a tiny, fast-moving woman of few words. She had high cheek bones, piercing eyes, and long grey hair she always wore up in a bun. She had an air of no-nonsense about her. My great-grandfather was tall and had a rather hard expression. He chewed tobacco, so his lips were often black and he was always spitting. Once I saw him pull my great-grandmother up onto his lap on the porch swing. It surprised me, as it was unusual to see them being so affectionate.

They were farmers, pure and simple, who spent their days literally eking out their daily bread and doing what was necessary for simple survival, as poor, rural, country folks did in the early part of the twentieth century. Joe was the sixth and last child to be born. But there was no doubt he would change life for all of them forever.

As I started digging more, questioning my mother and aunts, I discovered that Joe had never learned to speak or feed himself. One of my aunts recalled her most vivid memory was watching him pee off the porch. Just saying it made her wince. I learned as he approached adulthood, he became uncontrollable and the daily care overwhelming.

I picked up whispers that something had happened, some culminating, irrevocable event, leaving no doubt it was time for something to be done. And that something meant he'd have to be taken to an institution. Of course, as there was only a horse and buggy to make the occasional trips to town for supplies, they all knew what that meant. When the day came, I was told my tall, stern, great-grandfather wailed over the basin as he shaved. No one had ever seen him cry before.

Joe only lived a little over three years in the institution. The death certificate said he'd died of tuberculous. Yet, even in death he'd been placed apart, buried in a small church graveyard up the road from the house, not with the other family members who'd been buried in the much larger town cemetery.

Over the years, I've been left with a profound tenderness and compassion for my family and for the secret we've carried. How heartbreaking and challenging to the very brink it must have been caring for him every day: feeding as he became old enough to swipe a spoon, cleaning up after his random and perpetual incontinence, the smells, dressing and bathing. And in those days, having a child so clearly different would cast a long shadow of hiding and shame over all of them. I understood now why two of my great-aunts had never married until very late in life and one of my great-uncles had never married.

Still, I wondered when there'd been sweet moments, as I surely felt there must have been. Perhaps when he was very small, before his difference took hold or later, too, in some ordinary, unforeseen moments that can quickly take the heart by surprise. Was there someone in the family he was especially drawn to? Someone with whom he felt some safety—someone he knew would be there to catch his awkward fall? Did he ever have a favorite blanket or toy? Did he enjoy rolling, throwing, or catching a ball? Did anyone ever read him bedtime stories?

Unable to fully fathom the enormity of the secret, I kept peeling back every memory of my summer days there to see if I could find something, anything, any clue he'd once been a part of the family. But no. I found no dusty picture tucked in the back of the bottom drawer of the guest bedroom bureau. No mention of him in the yellowed papers crammed half folded in the nooks of the hall secretary. No token child's plate, bowl, or spoon left stored in a bottom drawer. Erased—except for the picture I'd found in my grandmother's cedar chest. Yet, now it seemed his darting presence peered at me from around every corner—a presence, as it turned out, that would not be forgotten.

I'll never know what irrevocable event led to Joe being taken away on that fateful day. I'll never know the depth of sorrow and, very likely, rage, they all tried to smother, make go away, but couldn't—couldn't even after he was gone. I just knew it was time for him to come out of that cedar chest.

A few years later, my first book was published, and it felt right to dedicate it to him. I included a short story about how I'd discovered his picture in the cedar chest but, before it went to press, I called my mom and aunts to let them know and to read the dedication. As they each listened quietly, I could hear the slow, soft tears coming. The long holding of the secret was, at last, giving way, making room for any chatter wanting to fill the newly opened space, once hidden and silent.

Yes, Joe's picture is still among the others in my grandmother's cedar chest but he is not. He's out now roaming free in their hearts . . . and mine.

Welcome home, Joe.

Miss Mammie Lee

During my visits each summer at my grandparents' house, Sundays meant goin'-to-church time. We'd get up early to make sure our best clothes were ironed and our hair curled. Dressed to perfection, we'd make our way over town in time for church.

My granddaddy had helped found the church, the Lauderdale Methodist Church, so his name was under one of the small windows, which I felt was pretty special. And, of course, like all the regulars, we had *our* special pew. All the pews were made of simple wood and could be a bit rickety when you sat down. Up front was a padded kneeling bench and a railing we'd use for taking communion. And hanging on the wall was one of those well-known pictures of Jesus—the one where he has long dark hair and he's gazing upward. Being a one-room church, there wasn't an organ but rather an old piano someone had donated. Some of the keys didn't play, and others would stick off and on, so when the piano player would fall behind a bit, well, we'd just all sing a little louder.

Sometimes there'd be a choir made up of maybe six to eight folks. Funny thing though, several couldn't carry a tune too well, and one dear woman, Miss Mammie Lee, liked to stand up front and sing the loudest. She'd always seemed to get started a little late, and her lone voice would ring in the silence after the music had stopped. When I was very young, I'd have to squeeze my belly tight and hold my breath to not burst out laughing!

Oh, but it'd be a lifetime before I could close my eyes and remember the slightly slivered feel of the rickety pew, hear the barely off piano keys, and see those choir faces only, this time, need to breathe in deep to hold the memories close. It's been especially poignant remembering Miss Mammie Lee with her imposing, unrestrained, and undiluted voice ringing out.

It stirs in me something so true as each time, with dutiful smiles of appreciation, we'd receive her most imperfect sounds again and again. Maybe it has something to do with how when it comes to worship, our simple self is quite enough. I don't know, but it seemed to me that by just being who she was and doing what she did, she taught all of us something about what was really important.

One Sunday when I was home from college, my grandmother and I got to go to church alone. On that day, the choir led us in the opening hymn, "How Great Thou Art," my grandmother's favorite. As we all stood, I put my arm around her shoulder, and together we sang it out—loud, with Miss Mammie Lee leading the way. And I could barely hold myself together. My grandmother had become such a light for me, especially since the passing of my granddaddy, and I knew I'd be etching out that short time deep into the most protected place I could possibly find for safekeeping.

Oh Lord, my God when I in awesome wonder consider all the worlds Thy hands have made, then sings my soul, my Savior God to Thee, how great Thou art . . . how great Thou art.

I know in these days of megachurches with their enamored buildings, organs, big professional choirs, and live music, such a memory of an old country church may feel a bit antiquated. True. Still, I'd give all the world for one more Sunday—to sit on the rickety seat-worn pew, to sing along with those sticky piano keys and, most of all, to hear Miss Mammie Lee's voice ring out loud and true.

I do believe it'd be an awesome wonder.

On the Screen Porch

I can still sense the soft winds in the live oak trees every time I return home to walk down the old roads where I was *raised up*, as they say. Though I was only there in the summers, it was home. Still is.

There, outside my immediate family, few knew I was a minister and even fewer knew of the Tree of Life. No matter. There, as mentioned earlier, I've always been known as something much more familial. And, truth be known, I've felt quite content to have it that way.

So, nothing could've prepared me for the night I arrived home to visit and settled into the rocking lounge on the screen porch. One of my aunts was now living in my grandmother's house, and my other aunt had come to visit. The three of us were sitting, chatting, enjoying the first hint of cool air and all the katydids and tree frogs now eager to chime in when suddenly . . .

"Someone's comin' up the drive!"

No! I thought, not wanting my sweet respite interrupted. But in they came, two of my aunt's friends and pillars of our hometown Methodist Church. The conversation was moving along with talk about all the current news when suddenly my visiting aunt said, "Well, you know Stephanie's a minister, and she's working on her doctorate."

My heart seemed to skip a beat and then was held still as I sensed that familiar feeling telling me to hold on—something was coming though I didn't know what.

"Really? Are you a Methodist minister?"

"No. I'm an Interfaith minister. I serve the Tree of Life Interfaith Temple in Amherst, New Hampshire."

An awkward silence.

And, I waited for the usual, "What's an Interfaith minister? Are you Christian?" But instead, one of our visitors asked, "What are you studying in school?"

Feeling it best to stay on semi-familiar ground, I said, "Well, I'm interested in the teachings of Jesus translated in Aramaic, the language he spoke. I've studied the Lord's Prayer in Aramaic and I'd like to expand on that."

Another silence.

And then, a look of curiosity. "Jesus was a Jew. Didn't he speak Hebrew?"

"Yes, of course, but his teachings in the Bible shared with everyday people are believed to have been spoken in Aramaic. Hebrew and Aramaic are thought of as sister languages, as they share a similar script."

A pause.

"Can you speak Hebrew?"

"A little. It's a beautiful language. I first studied it learning the Twenty-third Psalm."

"Oh, I love the Twenty-third Psalm. Could you say a few words in Hebrew?"

"Would you like to hear the whole psalm?"

"We'd love that."

Afterwards, this time, the silence that hung in the air was sweet, poignant, holding all of us together, resisting any temptation to be hurried along. And, then I heard, "Could you say the Lord's Prayer in Aramaic?"

"Sure."

And, again, afterwards . . . we were held sweetly, this time longer.

Though I was fully prepared to continue our conversation in whatever direction they would want to take it, perhaps to discuss Interfaith ministry or my broader research interests, this time, "My goodness, what a good job that young man did painting your house. You know, I need to get some work done on my house."

And as my aunt showed them around, "Hey, would y'all like a piece of banana cream pie? Was just made today."

"Absolutely!" And soon after they were gone.

It took me a while to fully grasp what had happened on the screen porch that night. It'd felt something like a window had been opened, gingerly, between my usually quite separate worlds. And for a moment they had breathed together. It'd left me with an odd sense of completeness that felt new and tender.

And it reminded me how effortlessly we can find one another when we pray together, particularly in those ancient languages that naturally create the silence . . . the silence so immune to words. For what is the need of words when we can sit together in that sweet, pulsing mystery—the mystery that holds all the world—and then, just as easily, go back to house painting?

After a week of fried green tomatoes, grits, collards, Southern fried chicken, and plenty of black-eyed peas, it was time to leave.

But this time I carried with me a memory of sitting still in the dark on that screen porch with those I barely knew, sharing together the mystery and, of course, some of my aunt's well-known banana cream pie.

And I left whole, complete, and shining.

4

Cracks in the Armor

Down Home

Take a walk down a woody road

one long forgotten
barely holding back sharp grasses and thorny vines

but leaves dust between your toes

Step slowly back . . . your feet will hear the old stories

Secrets . . .
the road is waiting to tell you

I'd heard Mini lived to be over a hundred and on her own until right before the end. I was grateful for that but wished she'd lived a bit longer to see what I know she could've never imagined. Me either back then.

For Mini

I could sit on my great-grandparent's porch in the deep Southern woods and count to ninety from the first time I could hear the faint sound of a car coming to finally seeing it round the curve just up the road. The sound was something like the hum the wind makes as it's first gathering strength. The old farmhouse sat back from the road, had a wraparound porch with a hanging swing on each end, and a peaked roof that jutted high into the sky. Behind the house was a large shed for the tractor and then, off to the side, tucked away, almost hidden in the tall bushes, was the outhouse.

No, we weren't the Antebellum South. We were the other South, poor but fiercely proud. My great-grandparents raised six children here, including Joe, in the early twentieth century. Pigs were hung upside down and slaughtered for bacon and salt pork, seedy watermelon was stolen away to the back fields on rare goofing-off-after-church-goin' afternoons, bottomless buckets of peas were shelled off the back steps, and the smells from the mid-day meal could linger well into the evening. We called it *down home*. It was deep in the country, about a half an hour from my grandparent's house. It was also where Mini would come to cook and clean for us.

Like other rural families with many children to feed and crops to plow, extra hands were needed in the house and fields. And those hands were black. Of course, by the time I was growing up and spending long, sweaty, days there, an image of those black hands in the fields could only be held alive in the vapors of memory. But Mini was no vapor. She was right there making those biscuits and then making my bed.

And so, she labored for our family for most of her long life. No doubt she loved us dearly, as we certainly felt so, and we always said we loved her *like* family. And, I believe, both were, undeniably true. As for me, however, living in a different part of the country most of the year, I didn't have the same history with Mini. So, while I was always happy to see her come through the back door (yes, only the back), mostly, I tried to turn away and not think about it too much. But, sometimes I couldn't and a sour feeling would start churning in my stomach.

I suppose I *could* have made it through without any unnecessary upheaval for those few weeks each summer. After all, this was where my roots were, the only place I knew I really belonged. And our stock was sturdy, the kind with solid backbones, straight gaits, and piercing eyes that could bore straight through the most unforgiving hardships of life. I loved them. And, of course, still do.

Yes, I suppose I *could* have, had it not been for that outhouse at the outer edge of the yard. Mini wasn't allowed to use the indoor bathroom. The outhouse was for her. One day, as I watched her heavy-laden ankles slowly carry her out to that outhouse, I could feel that churning again. But this time the inevitable tide having festered for what seemed like many summers could not be curtailed. I was old enough to feel it all but still too young to know what to do with it or where to put it. I just wanted it to go away. I wanted it to be different. So, this time, I waited for her to return and, finding us alone, blurted out, "Mini, why don't you use the indoor bathroom?"

And, exactly in that moment, I would have given my whole life to take it back. Her stunned, piercing glance felt volcanic, like hot embers, long dormant, now suddenly in real danger of erupting without regard to fallout. And I, in the wake, stopped breathing, paralyzed. Oh, but my young, naive, heart was screaming, *Mini, don't go out there! It's not right!*

Gratefully, her lifetime of well-adapted, this-is-how-you-behave-'round-whites instinct kicked in and she quickly recovered but not before giving me a good tongue lashing.

"You know better'in that Miss Stetnee. Things is how they is. You best leave it 'lone now!"

And turning from me, she threw the dry cloth over her shoulder and flashed me one last clear look of warning, "We be done w' this Miss Stetnee. We be done w' this." And so we were.

Things is how they is. My family would've said the exact same thing. Still, since, I've winced every time I remember. What *was* she to do with that? In truth, none of us, least of all me, not even yet a teenager, were equipped to do anything with, simply, yet regrettably, what was. It was more than what we did. It seemed to be who we were.

We never talked about it again. I returned home and, in later summers, would come to see Mini less and less, as age and health issues took hold of her. But over the years, I've often prayed that she knew what was in my heart that day and have longed to say to her . . .

Please forgive me. I couldn't watch you walk out to that outhouse again. I couldn't. Still, I'm sorry I was so unkind to you. I just wanted you to know I saw you . . . and so felt for you. I just didn't know how to say it. Oh Mini, thank you for your long, faithful, service to my family. Thank you for making the biscuits and our beds, and for caring for us. I'm just sorry we didn't know how to care for you . . . better.

And sometimes, through those vapors of memory, I can close my eyes and imagine us standing there in the kitchen again, her with that dry cloth flung over her shoulder and me now as a grown woman. But this time, from beyond the veil, she's gazing softly at me with an almost-smile.

An almost-smile holding that moment in the kitchen long ago, a moment filled with such ripped-open rage, regret, and shame . . . revealing a secret no longer sealed but couldn't be told by either one of us . . . yet still continues to whisper across time.

Bees and Jazz

We'd heard that *down home* had finally sold—this house and land that'd been in my family for almost two hundred years. I was relieved, as I'd seen it empty for a while and watched it steadily go down since the passing of my last remaining great-aunt, who'd lived in the house for many years. On recent visits, my heart would ache seeing the screen doors hanging off the hinges, paint peeling, windows covered with black paper, and always a scattering of garbage littering the porch. And the swing, the one that had silently joined me in my late afternoon musings, now hung crooked and still.

Holding fast to all the old faded photographs and to those lingering memories still alive in the vapors, I'd been asking my heart to let go, so I and this place, which had long held and sustained my family, could breathe in new life again.

Still, I couldn't have foreseen what was to come.

On what would be our last visit *down home*, my aunt, Doug, and I decided to drive by and see—but what, we didn't know. As we neared, we slowed down and saw a trailer parked in the front yard. Clearly, there was work being done on the house.

Suddenly, my aunt said, "Pull in the drive. I want to see who bought the house."

No! I thought. *Not a good idea. Maybe they'll think we're intruding.*

As we got out of the car and walked toward the trailer, a Black man wearing a blue print bandana and matching shirt came around the corner strolling casually toward us. As he got closer, we could see that his bandana loosely held back greying dreadlocks.

My aunt spoke first. "Hello . . . we'd like to speak with the owner."

A pause.

"I'm the owner." And I felt a silent gasp in my breath, some need to freeze the moment, to hold this unexpected brevity in time, one that held not just my life but so many lives before.

"Oh . . . well, this was my family's home for almost two hundred years. We'd heard it'd sold and wanted to stop by," my aunt said.

And I heard myself jump in.

"Looks like you're doing a lot of work on the house. When I was growing up, I used to sit on the porch and watch for cars to go by—on a swing that used to be over there," I said pointing toward the end of the porch.

"I actually bought the land first. I was taken by that field," he said, pointing in the opposite direction across the road. And it was then that a certain something in his voice let me know he was a perfect caretaker to help breathe new life into the place.

"It was my great-grandmother's favorite place to go in the early evening after supper," I said. And so, we chatted back and forth, our small talk soon effortlessly bridging across the depths of time, race, the old and the new.

At one point, a couple of bees came swarming around his head. "Don't worry," he said. "I'm a bee keeper," pointing to some crates nearby. "They won't bother you. They're mad at me because I moved them."

"Oh, it's okay," I said. "I know in time they'll be right at home here."

Then smiling, a surprise: "Would you like to come in?"

"Really?"

And, for the last time, we walked down the center hall—me holding fast to those vapors of memory. In the background, like a distant echo, I could hear him saying he was an electrician by trade and also a jazz musician. But then I was jolted back when he said, smiling again, "I'm redoing the kitchen first. I want it done before my family comes. We love to cook."

Oh, Mini, my heart prayed. *If you could only have known that some sixty years after that day in the kitchen a man would buy this house and that this kitchen would be filled with his family—all folks who love to cook . . . folks, dear Mini, who look just like you.*

Now when I think of *down home,* I think of bees, jazz music ringing across the wide-open field, and good smells coming from the kitchen. I think of new life arising out of the old. And I think of Mini and me, and I know somewhere deep down in my soul that we're both a little closer to being unburdened and free.

Stanley and Me

It couldn't have been more than ten minutes. We were passing by on an old country road when I caught a glimpse of him on a riding mower behind a small church not far from *down home.*

And on a whim, we stopped. I wanted to find out what I could about any of Mini's relatives who might still be in the area. As I walked toward him, he stopped the mower and came toward me. He was an older Black man, I'd say in his seventies, with a pleasant, welcoming face.

"Hello, sorry to bother you," I said reaching out to shake his hand and introducing myself. "I'm visiting from up north. My great-grandparents' home is not far from here, but it was sold recently. There used to be a woman who worked for my family for many years. Her name was Mini, and I believe she may have gone to a church around here. Any chance you may know of a Mini?"

"Mini?" he said with a hint of recognition. "If it's who I'm thinking it could be, she died a few years back. She was over a hundred but lived on her own till the end. But if it's her, her church would be just up the road."

"If it's her, you wouldn't happen to know if she has any relatives who might still be in the area? The last time I saw her I was a teenager. and I'd love to know what happened to her and something about her life."

He was silent for a moment and had a wondering look on his face.

"Well, let's see what I can do for you," he said pulling out his phone. "I know someone who might be able to help."

And as I stood there, I suddenly felt like we were very old friends. Whoever he was calling wasn't picking up so he left a message asking them to get back as soon as they could.

"Oh well," I said, "thanks so much for trying. What was your name?"

"Stanley." And then looking out across the road like he was trying hard to figure something out, "But you know, Baby, I sure wish I could help you."

The comment was filled with such simple sincerity, I felt more like his daughter standing there than some stranger. Later, it'd sink in that he'd called me *Baby*. And I thought about all the horrid history that could be hitched to such an endearing term—especially coming from a Black man to a White woman.

But on this day, off a backroad in the Deep South, we were just two people having a spontaneous conversation. His calling me *Baby* seemed to naturally hold, tenderly, the connection our short time together had created—a connection that lived well beyond race and the ravages of time.

And it gave me a kind of hope . . . hope for all humankind.

PART III

Discovery

5

The Soul's Imprint

Following the Joy

Turn slowly toward what leaves you silent
Hold fast to what makes you breathless

Stand empty

Longing's sweet fragrance will soothe your skin
even as Love's fire consumes you

Stand still
and Dance

Someone long ago asked me to write my epitaph. It's never changed. "She danced with God."

"Be Beautiful!"

When I was a young teenager, without a doubt, the most lifesaving, fun, I'm-at-home time was when I was in ballet class. There, once a week, I always felt free and happy like I could soar with Peter Pan! During the rest of the week, I'd often play dress up in my mom's old long skirts and dance around the apartment. I could do that for hours. But when I was in the accident I describe in *The Scar* and had the head injury, I was told it probably wasn't a good idea to dance due to the turning. I was devastated.

Then later, living in Hawaii with Dean, I found an adult ballet class in Honolulu. I thought it'd probably been long enough since the accident, so I anxiously decided to give it a try. Stepping into the second-story classroom with the worn wooden floor, hand-faded bars, and high open windows, my heart was pounding. How could it *possibly* get any better?

Oh my . . . but it did right when my teacher walked in. His name was Jack Clause and he definitely did *not* look like a ballet teacher or dancer. He was rather short and stocky, but his face—oh that face—held me fast. I'd soon learn you didn't come to class late. Always proper attire. No chit-chat. Yet, each week, I just knew something special was about to happen.

As we worked at the barre, he'd come around to each of us and say, "Up! Up! Up!" and he'd stand there until we were lifted and shining. Most importantly, he told us to *be beautiful* as we moved across the floor.

"Be beautiful!" he'd bellow. "There're many technicians but very few dancers! Be a dancer!" Now, most adult dancers, out of their prime and usually far from years of practice, often do *not* look so beautiful moving across the floor. But in Jack's class, I didn't care if I could do that grand jeté really high or not. Off I'd go as if I could fly! And it didn't matter how beautiful I looked, or didn't look, to others. Not on the radar. No, most importantly, it

46

was how I *felt* in his class, and afterwards too, as I continued to grand jeté down the sidewalk to catch the last bus home.

After a little over a year of dancing, we left Hawaii to spend a year overseas. It was during that time I realized the true gift of his teaching, and it felt very important to say *thank you*. I anxiously waited for the day we'd return home as I knew we'd be stopping for a few days in Honolulu. Finally, the day came when I found myself outside on the familiar sidewalk of the old building. At the top of the stairs, I asked the girl at the desk how I might get in touch with Jack. She stared at me awkwardly and asked, "You don't know?"

"Know what?"

"Jack died a few months ago. He had a heart condition. He knew he could die at any time. You didn't know? Most people knew." All I could do was shake my head and make my way back down the stairs, stunned and sad.

In the days that followed, I realized the even greater gift I'd received from his presence. I understood even more deeply why nothing less than *beautiful* was acceptable and why he wanted us to be *dancers*—not just technicians.

No time for chit-chat . . . indeed. Only time for beauty. And for doing what you love.

Thank you, Jack.

That Certain Something

Okay. I confess I rather enjoyed being not-so-discreetly perused by the slightly disapproving eyes of those around me—mostly notably from the older women, escorted by their distinguished husbands, drenched in their long furs, dawning freshly coiffured colored perms, and swaying those dangly earrings side-to-side with every move. All notable signs of those well-appointed and, of course, destined to sit in the front row of the mezzanine of the Mississippi Coast Coliseum that night in 1979 in Biloxi, Mississippi.

And then there was me, not so well-appointed, as I was *une*-scorted and *very* pregnant, arriving in my low-cut scarlet gown, loaned to me by a friend, and daring to sit in the front row, center seat. Now the low-cut part likely caused my most salacious grin, as I had only recently become quite voluptuous due to being pregnant. And I did have a pair of those dangly earrings to sway alongside my long, loosely hanging hair.

But while yes, I was enjoying some of the novel attention I was attracting, nothing could have detracted my mood which, by this time, was already in full aerobatic mode—leaping over the railing and down onto the stage where, very soon, I knew my heart would be dancing with Mikhail Baryshnikov. If this wasn't heaven, you couldn't have told me what was.

But, as I'd often discover, the great gift I received that night was even grander than Baryshnikov himself. You see, there had been some buzz about him being ill and even, perhaps, not being able to dance. Luckily, another great ballet dancer of the day, Peter Martins, was also there to perform.

So, the evening began with Martins. Having taken ballet and having danced in a small local company, the Pensacola Civic Ballet, the year before, I knew something about what I was watching. And Martins was absolutely *technically* brilliant. No question. Brilliant. But, then a short intermission and . . . there was Baryshnikov leaping through the air with such power and grace that we were all jolted up and out of our seats, gasping and clapping in response to some ubiquitous, primal, involuntary force.

As I watched throughout the evening, I could see that, at least on this night, Baryshnikov was not as technically brilliant as Martins. But it didn't seem to matter because Baryshnikov just had that . . . *certain something*. Now I could imagine that, on other nights, Martins too exuded that *certain something*, also being a very celebrated dancer. But this night, to me, clearly belonged to Baryshnikov.

We all recognize that *certain something* when we see it. It certainly exists in all the great ones who've spent years honing a craft to technical brilliance to suddenly discover their craft doing them. Still, as I experienced in my dance class with Jack, even if I hadn't spent years doing ballet, I could still step joyously into that *certain something* by fully letting go into my love of it.

It's been fifty years since I saw Jack's beaming face that sparked that *certain something* in me. Yet it's like it was yesterday. This tells me that that *certain something* is eternally alive, woven intrinsically into our DNA forever pointing us toward our true love . . . and when we have the courage to fully let go into its force, we too can quite *ahhhh*mazingly find it, life, doing us. And, we . . . well, we're just along for the ride.

And we discover how a few grand jetés down a Honolulu sidewalk could stir a magic to last a lifetime.

Spiraling Home

We'd heard a lot of students stayed away from Fr. Robert VerEecke's sacred and liturgical dance summer intensive at Boston College. Something about the assignment to *dance your God* had left even the most devout faint of heart.

But again, the most profound experience of that summer of 2004 was not in the culminating event but, actually, in another one. There were some students in our class who had cerebral palsy and were in wheelchairs. Each had a helper to assist. One afternoon, Fr. Bob, as we called him, announced we'd be put into pairs and given a line from a psalm to dance over a period of about two minutes. We'd only be given a few minutes to be with our partner to decide on an approach. He purposefully didn't give us a lot of time to think about it or to plan it all out.

I was paired with one of the men with cerebral palsy. During the few minutes we were given to prepare, I sat quietly close by. I really didn't know what else to do, as there was nothing in my experience to draw from. Literally, I was blank. There was no possibility for discussion or collaboration, not even the possibility of eye contact, which might offer some confirmation we were in sync. And his helper was silent.

When it came time for us to dance, I stood motionless and tried hard not to stare at his frail, twisted body or to respond to his moaning sounds. Then, somewhere in the background, I heard Fr. Bob say, "Just dance. Only punctuate with key words as the spirit moves."

Just dance, I thought. There's literally nothing else to do.

Then, I remembered, *what's the same in all of us*—something I'd been seeing, hearing, sensing, cultivating in seminary. And in the eternal fullness of what was only a second or two, I found my home inside and something lifted. Suddenly, I could *see* this beautiful soul. I took a deep breath and stepped out toward him not knowing where it would lead. His helper responded and soon we were moving out across the floor, forward, back, turning, pausing, fast, slow. And as I *heard* my partner's sounds, I joined in, mingling my own sounds and words, in and out, in and out, and together we created our own language as we were carried, spiraling, into some void where all stood perfectly still—and *we* were the dance.

I don't even remember his name. But I came to know him in a way I've been blessed to know few others. Our souls danced together that day, the *what's the same in all of us,* beyond all personal or individual differences. And it sparked a joy inside, still and quiet, I carry to this day.

Splash!

It was just another birthday. Not a decade or even a midway marker, so I decided a casual dinner at a restaurant close by, one we could walk to, would suffice. Funny thing about getting older, now in the last category of those age-range listings—you know, the roughly twenty to forty, forty to sixty-five, and then just sixty-five+. That plus sign's a poignant reminder that from that point on, no one really knows, can't even predict.

Of course, none of us can at any time. And I certainly feel fortunate and blessed to have arrived at that last category. But a surprise waits there, poking uninvited through the rote passing of days and nights. Now I *know*, viscerally, that each sunrise signals one less to go, and each sunset seals away what has passed with no promises for retakes or redos.

It's not about dying. I actually think that'll be quite the ultimate adventure. It's more about leaving behind all the possibilities—for tender glances with those I love, Doug's hand on the small of my back as we cross the street, fighting back fear to speak my truth, sending silent care to the stranger sleeping on the street corner, pausing to hold close the sound of the mourning doves cooing into the sky, making amends, smelling that aged woodsy scent when we first open our off-the-grid cabin door, getting to see my amaryllis bloom again—all such possibilities no longer possible.

"*Carpe diem!*" whispers the dead poet. Indeed.

Such were the musings circling my heart as Doug and I made our way to the restaurant on that balmy, breezy night, perfect for our early evening stroll. Arriving at the restaurant, we were seated at a table tucked away in a side corner and enjoyed a scrumptious meal. Perfect. Until we got up to leave. Walking toward the door, we could barely see outside for the torrential rain coming down sideways.

Four blocks from home, staying dry wasn't an option. Wasn't going to happen. Our first thought was to just wait it out. Then, "NO!" I said, "It's my birthday! Let's go!" And like a kite catching the wind, out I went, turning my face right into the thick whipping rain, and Doug followed. Soon I was stomping in every puddle along the way, side to side, teasing and chastising the rain for trying to wilt my giggles. Splash! *Yahoooo!!*

I was somewhat aware of the stares we were getting from strangers huddled under store awnings and from others in passing cars. Didn't matter. I couldn't stop laughing, stomping, galivanting. Some seventy years had just fallen away and I was four years old again. Oh, how I didn't want it to end.

On that just-another-birthday, I got to be a kid again, to play, be silly, get drenched, and dance in raindrops without a care in the world. And, you know, I imagine at the end of my days, if fortunate enough to have time to look back over my life and share with others, one thing I'll definitely say with a giggle is, "Hey, do you remember my seventy–fourth birthday—the one when we walked home in the rainstorm? Now *that* was the best birthday ever."

6

The Sound of God

Getting Tuned

Caught
Breathless
Remembering . . . forgetting

Like a bell echoing on a summer breeze, each sound calls me home
and, together, sing softly, chiming in the wind . . .

a kind of lullaby known only to the Beloved

And I . . . I am rocked to sleep . . . even as I am waking

And God found me just beyond my mind's meanderings . . . in that silence that followed my noisy, yearning prayers.

Half a Second

No! I was *not* happy. I'd been chanting a beautiful version of Psalm 23 in Hebrew in my spiritual practice for some time. I was so in love with it that one day, early on when I was still memorizing, I couldn't pull myself out of my car in a Walmart parking lot. Impossible. Shopping would have to wait!

So, when my Hebrew teacher suggested I take up a different practice, Genesis 1:1–3 in Hebrew, *and* learn it from a recording of a well-known rabbi in order to receive the full imprint of the Hebraic and Jewish lineage, well, I was *not* happy. But over the years I'd learned, especially when feeling deep resistance, if I could give myself to a practice, I'd often discover something unexpected, even beautiful, on the other side.

And so, begrudgingly, I put aside my Psalm 23 and started listening to a recording of Genesis 1:1–3 given to me by my teacher. Every morning I'd wake up and make my way to my special place to begin. And every morning my mind would come right along in full-complain mode. *I don't like this! His voice is raspy! Why am I such a good do-be? Maybe I'll do my Psalm 23 afterwards. No. Stop! Give it a chance!* But my mind would go on and on like some well-rehearsed chorus chiming in the background behind the lead singer—in this case, me. Even in the silence that followed, that special holy place, the very portal to all beyond understanding, my mind would continue to echo in complaint.

This continued for several weeks. Then, one morning, maybe because my mind was exhausted or, more likely, because the initial memorizing had finally given way to the flow of the sound current, something happened . . . in that sweet silence that follows. Suddenly, it was like a shutter opened for how long I don't know—but felt like no more than half a second—and then closed again. Startled, I was immediately snapped back to normal consciousness. But it left me jarred and still inside for quite some time.

There've only been a few times over my many years of practicing what I call Mantra Prayer that I've experienced that half a second. I've come to call such times of full immersion into the One *love's kiss* because they've made a lover out of me—a lover who knows instantly a kiss from her Beloved. Graciously, these times are recognizable only in hindsight because when I'm *in* them I'm no longer observing them. In those half-seconds, there's no distinction between me as a separate person and what's moving across the screen of my mind's imagination.

It's something like what Kabir meant when he offered that we all know a drop merges into the ocean, but few of us know that the ocean merges into the drop. In full immersion, I'm not feeling like a drop in the ocean or simply imagining myself being a part of the ocean. No. I *am* the ocean. And on returning, experiencing myself as a drop again, I'm reminded I'm made of something bigger, much bigger, infinite, than I could ever wrap my finite brain around. How can I be sure?

I've been the ocean.

I've been kissed.

The Unexpected Blessing

And sometimes Mantra Prayer cracks me open. It happened in a living room of a large old home in Cambridge, Massachusetts, where I was gathered with my Sufi Sangha, a part of Sufi Ruhaniat International. We were studying and practicing the mystical teachings of Sufism as well as learning the beautiful Dances of Universal Peace. The dances were particularly captivating, as there I found my love for chanting, movement, and prayer effortlessly and sweetly intermingled, merged into one.

So, though primed for beauty, I wasn't prepared for what was coming—a new dance called "I Am Blessed":

> I am blessed by your presence Oh Lord. I am filled with
> your blessings Allah.
> *La il la il Allah . . . La il la il Allah . . . La il la il Allah . . .*
> *Ya Allah.*

Slowly, turning and chanting, I reached my right palm up to the sky to receive the Holy Spirit as I pointed my left palm toward the floor, imagining heaven and earth becoming one at my heart center.

La il la il Allah means there is nothing more worthy of praise than Allah and, realizing this, all we see is Allah, Allah being Arabic for God. I'd heard this translation many times, but on this day, turning slowly, eyes closed, I somehow *became* the beautiful Arabic sounds, and the tears poured down my softly smiling face—not tears of joy or even wonder—but of something well beyond both.

Similar to that first experience at Asilomar years ago, the tears flowed from some infinite, neutral, quiet, fully complete place, whole unto itself—and, in this case, me. For in that breathing, sounding, stepping, turning, eternal moment, there was only God. What before I'd only understood, *now* I knew. What before I could've described quite succinctly, *now* had made me wholly silent.

For many days following, I could be out in the world looking for that special spice for my spaghetti sauce, washing a sweater to lay flat to dry, paying bills, talking to a neighbor, listening to the mourning doves hovering close out our window—didn't matter, everywhere and always there was only God.

Over time, I came to add . . . Yes, there is only God . . . *if* we have the eyes to see, the ears to hear, and the heart to know . . . as this was the only way I could create within myself the possibility to see, hear, and know the divine essence in *all* my brothers and sisters, particularly beyond the angst, hatefulness, and all the horrific behaviors that occur.

Yes, *La il la il Allah* opened me to recognize we're each sinner and saint, human and divine, and over time it's helped me to be less quick to judge the human and quicker to recognize the divine, sometimes very camouflaged, standing right there in front of me.

And every now and then, when I pause and remember *La il la il Allah*, my footsteps slow and my vision changes, becoming soft, and I can *see* beyond what is visible, *hear* beyond what is spoken, and *know* what only our common heart knows—we're each totally messy, disheveled, cracked, worn, full of despair, rage and sorrow—*and* we are each fully whole, complete and shining unto ourselves and God.

And, in such moments, I am . . . truly . . . blessed.

The Dove's Feather

At the core, Mantra Prayer is always about joy. Sometimes when I'm struggling, feeling overwhelmed by what seems like an onslaught of crushing feelings to my fledging spirit, I know it's time for serious action. Enough!

One such time, I decided to take myself out for one of those long walks in a nearby park. I put on my favorite pink sweatshirt, the one with black letters "amour" (French for love) and a rose on the front, pulled on my comfy cutoff jeans, and slipped into my favorite walking shoes. Last, I grabbed my iPod and headphones.

As I started out, I decided to play "Sing Allelu," an ancient Christian hymn. It's a surefire go-to because *Ah* is the sacred sound used to connect with the One, called by many names. Christians sing Alleluia praising Abba, Aramaic for father. Jews call out to Yahweh, O God of Israel. Muslims chant *La il la ha il la Allah,* an extended version of the *La il la il Allah,* declaring Allah to be the only God. Hindus intone Atman, the universal God-self of each person.

As I steadily picked up speed, I could barely hold myself back from skipping. Now, when I walk, I'm somewhat aware of those around me, as I do tend to sing along with my music. But on this day, I didn't care much. And then, about ten minutes in, I saw a feather out in front of me. Small but not possible to miss. *Ah,* but this was no ordinary feather. It was a dove's feather.

Feeling most certain I'd struck gold—or, even better, a chord with the Holy Spirit—there was no holding back now! My heart did "open wide to see Your face"—now everywhere before me! From the ones passing who looked at me smiling to others who simply looked away. No matter. Now, I could see the face of the Holy Spirit everywhere. Even the stone people, tree spirits, high-flying hawks, and the still, cool, canal waters had joined in.

"Sing Allelu . . . Sing Allelu . . . We rejoice in Your love most high, in Your Light You shine forever, shine in us O Lord forever, we're the light to the world . . . Allelu!"

Suddenly, all the world was singing, and I allowed myself to be moved along by the gathering breeze, guided now by the feather directing, compelling my every step. For my beloved feather had become something like a conductor's baton, as I, now full of fervor, imagined directing all those who could to rise up and join in the chorus—to sing out loud and free—"We're the light to the world, Allelu!" Yes! *We're* the light to the world, you and I, right here and now, in the park, in the subway, in a crowd, in our solitude, in our laughter, in our tears, in the depths of challenge and suffering, in the very midst of joy and gratitude. No matter who we are, where we are, or what may be happening in our lives or beyond, *we* are still, unequivocally, unmistakably, unapologetically, the *light* to the world!

And I could feel my feather directing those gathering winds to move across time and space to gently wisp up against all who were suffering, soothe the unnameable, calm the heart spasms, restore peace to those too weary to get up, and deliver a love song to all who'd forgotten how to sing . . . so each weary, humble heart could find its song again.

Thank you, blessed dove, for your feather and for the power of the Holy Spirit it brought reminding me, us, we are each, indeed, the light of the world and remembering, we, most blessedly, can raise up one voice and . . .

Sing Allelu!

A Power-Love Song

Hum Bah De Lo Ah . . . Hum Bah De Lo Ah . . . Hum Bah De Lo Ah . . . Hum. I'd just turned the sharp corner down the long drive of our wilderness camp, 3 Feathers, when this chant dropped into my soul. I'd been sending prayers on the wind of the Great Spirit, asking for my power song to be sung through me, one I could use to commune more deeply with the spring waters, leafy friends and roaming animals on our mountain. Still, it so took me by surprise, this song-chant I'd never heard before, I rushed back to our cabin to write it down, thinking I might look up its meaning. (And the Great Spirit was smiling.) Of course, I couldn't find any such chant or even anything remotely like it. This is because our power song is a unique expression of our soul. Pause. Imagine that.

For thousands of years, holy men and women from indigenous cultures have gone out into nature to *hear* their power songs, songs used for healing and ceremonial work. It's less known that each of us, as well, carries a song, one that silently waits in the deep crevasses of our heart yearning to one day escape, free—singing. I like to call it a power *love* song because its power engenders a deep connection to all of life.

Now, each time we visit 3 Feathers, I take my drum or rattles and go out singing my power love song into the Spirit of the Place. And sometimes when I stop and become very still, I can feel its song, its love, in return. And, together, our song fills my soul as my spirit, and the Spirit of the Place, become one.

Would you like to find your song so your soul can sing again? If so, leave the known way and follow the path known only to the hidden salamander, budding sunflowers, underground caverns, and the night stars lingering, shining just for you, from a lost time. It will arise from the Great Mother into your feet as your heart instinctively propels it out, singing onto the breath of the Great Spirit to bless all on your path. And you will know a joy that comes releasing all you carry not essential to the beauty and goodness of life.

And, your soul will hear . . . hear now . . . the silent song, humming between each sound, birthing you into the Soul of the World.

7

The Other Realms

Finding God Beyond the Veil

You leaped into my heart when you didn't know I was looking
and now my Soul has become your playground.
Suddenly, I am unable to stop grinning
and this spring in my step is attracting attention.
You, my deer, have completely taken me over
and I remain clueless in joy with you . . .
unable to fathom the blessed fate of my captivity.
Possessed by you, I am set free.
In the silent wonder of you, I sing aloud.
And now, in the heart of you,
I soar.

Signed,
Clueless

"Come," said the Great Spirit. "I, in all my forms, am waiting to gift you with a love you've yet to know."

Unripe Fruit

In *Flight* I mentioned the eagle's head carved into the tip of a deer's antler that Doug had said called to him for me. Just like I'd never heard him talk like that before, I couldn't have imagined where I would soon be led—on a wondrous journey into the other realms all around us and within us, realms that have been known to holy men and women, from indigenous cultures around the world, for thousands of years.

In one of those realms, known in shamanist cosmology as the Lower World, I found my eagle and deer waiting to gift me with unconditional love. In another realm known as the Upper World, I found teachers and guides, some of whom you'll meet in coming stories, eager to walk side by side with me. And finally, in the realm known as the Middle World, the spirit side of this creation, I'm continuing to explore what Dr. George Washington Carver knew: how to talk to the flowers, hear the earth's healing whispers, and commune with the silent call of the grasshopper.

But in the early 1990s I knew nothing of such things, as I anxiously made my way, along with a couple of friends, to my first shamanism workshop offered in Boston by Michael Harner and Sandra Ingerman. We were taught how to journey, as they called it, to the other realms. In one of the first journeys, I held the intention to receive the name for my new yoga studio and, sure enough, it came: The Tree of Life.

At one point, we were invited to dance our spirit power animals, and I, of course, being a lover of dance, dove right in. Off I went and can still remember the freedom that instantly filled my soul as first the Spirit of the Deer and then the Spirit of the Eagle began to move my body. Carried, held, opened . . . and up and off I went into unknown parts of myself.

Traveling home that day, I was quite sure I'd found a new path I knew I wanted to know much more about. I started taking other workshops and reading all I could get my hands on. One of the books was *Native Healer: Initiation into an Ancient Art* by Medicine Grizzly Bear Lake. Absolutely every word spoke to me.

Round the same time, Doug and I had started camping in the wilds of Maine during our summer vacations. This was entirely new to me, as I'd never even been tent or campground camping. But after the first trip, and discovering a special spot hidden deep in the wilderness, I was hooked.

And then . . . all of these timely experiences: receiving my eagle head carved from a deer antler, finding out they were my spirit power animals, being given the Tree of Life name for my business, falling in love with the wilderness, and especially reading *Native Healer* all conspired to propel me to make a decision I was sure was coming directly from the Great Spirit. I'd write Medicine Grizzly Bear Lake and ask him to take me on as his shaman's apprentice, as I was quite certain I was called to be a shaman. Of course, I needed to point out I could only do this part-time because, after all, I was teaching at the University of Maine in the behavioral sciences, was married, and had two small children. Ha!

I still cringe when I think of it! Gratefully, he actually wrote back and was very kind, likely sensing my sincerity yet total unpreparedness for even asking for, much less taking on, such a venture. He described the years he'd lived with his teacher, serving in basic ways in exchange for the teachings he'd received, and made some recommendations for further study.

No, I wasn't happy, but reading his letter, I found myself feeling quite relieved he hadn't sent me out on some extended vision quest excursion designed to teach me a lesson! Later, I shared this story in my first book and sent him a copy.

And after all these years, I'm happy to report I'm still ripening.

Deer's Blessing

It was one of those mornings I'd awakened feeling absolutely fabulous. Glorious. All was right with the world. Even the colors of the flowers in our garden seemed to be glowing extra bright in the morning sun.

I was planning to work on my dissertation, particularly on a section I was having trouble with. So, I decided to do a shamanic journey to ask for help. By this time, I'd come to rely on the support and guidance I'd always found in the other realms from my spirit animal helpers and guides, as well as from the elemental spirits in nature. I knew them as different forms of God.

But in my journey, the Spirit of the Deer came. This felt odd to me, as she'd always made a habit of showing up almost exclusively when I was in need of some kind of healing. As I was feeling particularly good, I was truly perplexed as to why she was there. But there she was, hovering over me, licking my face. She seemed very playful and would not leave no matter how much I insisted.

I love you, my deer, I responded in kind, *but I don't need you this morning. I'm looking for help with my writing.* But she kept licking my face and would not stop. Finally, I gave up and ended the journey. Knowing nothing that comes from the other realms, particularly from a spirit power animal that's been with me for many years, is by chance or accidental, I wondered what it was all about.

A couple hours later, I felt the first odd pain in my lower belly. Shortly after, another. I got down on the floor and did some exercises, thinking that would help. It didn't. Now the pains were starting to intensify. Finally, I called my doctor's office. It's rare that an actual person answers. Usually, I'd hear a recording, leave a message and have to wait, sometimes hours, for a triage nurse to call. But on this morning, I heard a woman's voice. I described my discomfort and she said simply, "Go to the emergency room now." It was early afternoon.

At the hospital, I was examined and quickly sent for an ultrasound. The waves of pain were now so intense, I'd been given medication. Finally, in the early evening, the ultrasound was read and the doctor told me, quite seriously, he was assembling a surgical team. By this time, I was barely cognoscente of what was happening. I do remember, though, the nurses and doctors rushing around and my asking why everyone was in such a hurry. No one answered.

The next morning, I woke in a hospital room. When the doctor came, he told me a piece of scar tissue had wrapped around my large intestine, causing a bowel blockage. The rhythmic pain was the waste trying to push through and, not being able to, building up. Later, I'd learn I was very close to death, as my intestines were on the verge of bursting.

"You were lucky," the doctor said.

No. I thought to myself as I smiled politely. *You see, I had an omen yesterday morning. My deer came to let me know I'd be okay.*

This experience shifted something deep inside of me. I made some important changes to create more space for birthing vision-dreams I knew were calling. Mostly, though, when I think of it, I remember the blessed Spirit of the Deer . . . and the full message I'd received . . .

You're going to be fine but time is short. Play. Love. Create.

Eagle's Gift

It's true. We *had* known for a while that the day would come. Ever since *our* beloved site had become protected by the Maine land trust (yes, I know it's a good thing) and the road out to the site was cleared, actually making it passable by car (what *were* they thinking?) We'd known. Still, I wasn't prepared.

On our first day, after settling into our other home away from home, The Pines Lodge and Camps on Sysladobsis Lake, we excitedly made our way out to our site—the one we'd discovered years ago on our first trip into the Maine wilderness and the one to which we'd returned ever since. We'd become fond of calling it *our* site, as it was so remote, and it seemed no one was ever there but us, that is until it'd recently become protected by the Maine land trust and had even become domesticated with a picnic table. (I was *not* happy.) So, walking in on the tree-covered, moss-laden path, I found myself holding my breath a bit, hoping no one else would be there. *Whew!! Lucked out!*

Hello magnificent pines! I see more little ones are catching up! Oh, how I've missed you, beloved pond—your sacred, deep waters. I'm here again to play and frolic and be cleansed in your holy depths. Mr. Turtle? Are you still here guarding the Spirit of these waters?

And then I noticed a small log book chained to the picnic table. The last entry read, "Here with my five-year-old son. Great spot for fishing. Beautiful." And my heart paused with some unfamiliar, just awakened yet unformed knowing of things. It was a tender, kind omen.

The next day we got up early to head back out to our site. But, when we reached the end of the logging road, we saw a trailer. *Okay,* I thought. *They're probably fishing at the stream.* But, as we walked through the woods and our site came into view, we saw a tarp and a cooler. My heart sunk, really sunk, deep into some unknown cavern where all I could hear bouncing off the walls was, *Noooooooo!* and soon after, *what if they're here the whole week and we don't get to come back?*

Later that day I went for a long walk and a swim at The Pines and tried to let it all sink in. I confess there was some part of me feeling a bit silly for how I was taking it all. Most assuredly, all my long study of Eastern notions about non-attachment and non-permanence had just, unceremoniously, flown right out the window. *Total nonsense!* I wailed. There was no way I was going to pull myself up from the depths of my sorrow-filled caverns on the ropes of such lofty, ethereal, spiritual precepts. No! This was serious!

Then, laying on the dock, "Here with my five-year-old son. Great spot for fishing. Beautiful." And something started to clear. That night we had dinner with others staying at The Pines but I was quiet inside, needing to let this *we knew it would happen one day* event settle into its rightful place in my bones.

The next morning, sitting on our porch, a bald eagle flew down right in front of us and landed in a nearby tree. It must have paused there for several minutes as if to make sure his message was being delivered. It was. The Spirit of the Eagle comes, in this world or as my spirit power animal in the other realms, when I need to be reminded to soar high, to broaden my view, and to see beyond the surface of things. And as I closed my eyes, I could see a father and his little boy fishing, happy, and enjoying the pond in all its sacred beauty—in a way known only to them.

And, through my tears, my heart smiled.

On our last day, the folks at our site had (most graciously) left, and we got to spend a full glorious day there. And I wrote in my journal to secure its memory and place in my grateful, will-love-you-forever heart . . .

> Hanging limbs help me down the steep slope as the sound of You, rushing free, draws me in. I pause and ask the Spirit of the Turtle for permission. Then, leaving my clothes, I slowly step in, and I'm soon submerged by the still cool waters. And I am born again. Your rotting stumps and jutting limbs guide my passage for, yes, here, You are as dangerous as You are beautiful. Yet, in this place, stripped down of all trappings, I feel bold and untamed like You. I lay back on Your altar, and I am

baptized, once again, by the cool waters of Your grace. And, unbound by all I have been or will be, I am set free. As I rest on Your pine-needled, soft ground, I can feel the Spirit of You seeping into me as I watch Your tree limbs dance against the wide blue endless sky—these trees I have long loved since first finding them fledging upwards in green wonder all those years ago.

But now, the sun is making its way down in Your darkening sky. It's time to go. But my heart prays . . . prays from the very core of me . . . alive and pulsing with the heart of You:

Thank you . . . Spirit of this Place for all the ways you have gifted me, us, for so long.

Thank you . . . Spirit of the Eagle, for only on your wings could I have been lifted from the caverns of despair to soar with you . . . Only on Your wings could I have been made to see what You see . . . a father and his little boy and two fishing poles . . .

And be able to say with a heart overflowing . . .

Welcome! I'm so glad you're here.

Owl's Message

Six years after starting the Tree of Life Yoga Studio in a lovely building just off our town oval, I knew I desperately needed more room. Right next door was the perfect space, but it'd long been rented as an antique store, and the business owner showed no signs of leaving. I hadn't wanted to move from my ideal location, as I'd also cultivated a very close relationship with my landlord's family. It felt something like I was leaving home. But I needed more space. So, sadly, I started looking into other locations.

Finally, I found a very large, third-floor space that overlooked a river. Though there was no elevator, which was not ideal, the building was a historic old mill which also housed many small arts and crafts businesses and entrepreneurs. It had a good vibe.

On the day I was to sign the lease, I noticed a large barn owl sitting on a tree limb in our backyard. Hours passed, and still he sat motionless. As I knew owls were often the bearers of omens, I wondered what the message might be. Then, late morning, as I was about to leave to meet my new landlord, I got a call that my mom was having health problems, and I knew I needed to fly down south right away. Though there was still time to go sign the lease before catching my flight, for some reason, I chose not to. Instead, I left a phone message for my soon-to-be landlord saying I'd be in touch on my return and would finalize things then.

And still the owl sat motionless. Shortly before leaving for the airport, I walked outside and paused one last time to look up at him.

"Hello, Mr. Owl," I said.

And then, as if to answer, he lifted one of his wings up and then down—the first movement I'd seen all day.

"Thank you for being here. What is your message?" Again, he lifted his wing up and down. Still, I wasn't at all sure what the message could be.

When I returned home a week later, there were a number of messages on my answering machine. Among them was one from the owner of the antique store.

"Hey Stephanie. This is Rachael. Just wanted you to be the first to know that I'll be leaving this month. I'm moving my business over to the coast."

Now I understood why I'd decided not to rush off to sign the lease before catching my flight. Owl had come to deliver the omen, to tell me to remain still, right where I was, as he did . . . to wait, to trust. Feeling quite ambivalent about moving to the new space, Owl had come to remind me I didn't have to settle for what didn't feel absolutely right. For when we know to whom it is we belong, and we want nothing more than to do the work of our beloved God, why wouldn't we be given all the most optimal conditions within which to do so?

Indeed, why not?

Thank you, Spirit of the Owl.

PART IV

Valleys and Mountain Tops

8

Playing in the Valley

Sweet Delights

Diamond sparkles
dancing light
on lapping waves of deep blue grey

Come play!
Step into me . . . try and catch me!
Here I am!

Yes
between
Just as I disappear

And set your Soul ablaze

In the *Introduction: When the Katydids Went Silent*, I mentioned that one of the great gifts of Religious Science was that the church taught me about prayer, specifically how to cultivate a deep faith, belief, in my connection to God, who was speaking a common language through all the great faiths, mystics, and holy ones. In addition, on a practical level, it introduced me to a type of prayer process helpful in connecting with this one God to manifest everyday desires.

The short version was we were simply to write down in the present tense what it was we were wanting, affirm it was already happening, and then put it into a drawer or somewhere for safe keeping. In this way, God could respond in the most perfect way and time. Years later, I'd hear a lot about this process in discussions around the Law of Attraction and, more recently, in descriptions of similar programs promising all sorts of mind-expanding capabilities.

I fully embraced those early Religious Science teachings because I knew, mostly, at a very deep level, that if God could save me from that terrible abyss, speak for me when I could not, well, I just knew he could do anything. Faith wasn't something I had to reach for. Faith had already become who I was. So, I learned early on not to fret over the details of how things might come about—instead, to focus on the *what* and leave the *how* to God.

It's fun. Magical. Beautiful. But the danger can be that you may think you've arrived at the final summit, the mountain top, when you're actually just playing in the valley. The valley is the home of the ego, both healthy and unhealthy. But the ego is only capable of taking you to the base of the mountain. To travel further up, to where the deeper treasures of awe, silent wonder, surprise, and grace reside, the ego must stay behind, for the mountain top is home to only the fully surrendered soul. We'll get there, but first let's have some fun in the valley!

"You're a Witch!"

During the time Dean and I were living in Hawaii, I thought it'd be good to work on a master's degree. I was drawn to psychology and counseling because I could feel so many empty and lost parts inside of me. Yes, I had a deep faith and trust in my God, but I didn't have peace. I was always hiding behind some sense of perfection as a way to keep me out of harm's way. Remember from *Freed* that I was a good girl. I had no clue how to just be me—or any idea what that actually meant.

Unfortunately, my college grade point average was only a 2.78, and my GRE score was so low as to be embarrassing. I'd spent much of my early school and college years coping with the anxiety of oh-my-gosh-will-I-have-to-speak-today, which, of course, is an integral part of most academic courses, I rarely focused long enough to take in information. I routinely slipped by with barely passing grades. So, after I'd applied and been turned down by the University of Hawaii and all the other possible schools on the islands, I knew it was prayer time. I wrote down that I wanted a master's degree program in psychology or counseling and put it in the drawer. I prayed daily and released it out for manifestation.

It wasn't long before Dean came home one night smiling, handing me a flyer and said, "You're a witch!" The flyer announced a new master's degree program, specifically for military personnel and their dependents, offered right there on the base, in psychology, counseling, and guidance from the University of Northern Colorado! It was an excellent program, as many of the professors were at the top of their field, earning a very desired teaching assignment in Hawaii. And the program allowed for a lot of autonomy in creating papers, assignments, and projects. So, when I graduated with a 3.77, I felt, happily, for the first time, that just maybe, I was smart.

Midnight Coffee Spill

Recall in *Be Beautiful!* that after our tour in Hawaii, Dean was assigned to an overseas deployment. It was to Iwakuni, Japan. Though the tour was designated as unaccompanied, I and several other wives had decided to go independently.

I was excited to immerse myself in the culture, and since English had been my major in college, I imagined I could volunteer as a tutor to teach English as a second language. Though I didn't know a word of Japanese, I was certain I could find a way to make it work.

Dean kept assuring me that, this time, it wasn't possible. As I would be there independently, he couldn't see how any such opportunities might present themselves. In truth, I couldn't either. But, as I mentioned earlier, I'd learned not to fret over the details of *how*. So, I wrote my prayer, and into the drawer it went.

It was around midnight when our transport plane landed at a small hangar in what seemed like the middle of nowhere. Inside there was a couple sitting at a table drinking coffee. They'd soon be leaving on our plane. We joined them.

"So, how'd you guys like it here?"

I listened eagerly as the woman, who'd also been there independently, described her experience. They'd rented a house off base and encouraged us to do the same filling in many details about how to navigate daily life. Then, as it was time for them to board, the woman said, "The only regret I have is that I wasn't able to find anyone to take my part-time English teaching position."

Dean, who'd just taken a sip of coffee, gasped and almost dropped his cup, spilling some of the coffee! She went on to give me all the information. I was to contact a Mr. Oshima at the American English Academy. She said they were always looking for volunteers to tutor and teach English to the children after the regular school day.

It turned out to be an amazing year. I was blessed to be in very welcoming homes where I tutored the children. One family lived at the top of a very steep hill. I rode a bicycle, and as I was about to arrive at the top, the children would run out to greet me cheering me on for the last stretch. When it'd be time to leave, the mother and children would stand outside and wave to me as I peddled back down the hill.

Some of the parents could speak English but most only sparingly. Interestingly, the lack of a common language was not a barrier. In retrospect, I believe our connections were palpable because, in some ways, language was not in the way. With only the silence between us, our gestures, expressions, subtle glances, and knowing smiles had to take over. And, with that, I discovered how God could easily fill the spaces between us with only the essentials of the heart.

A Look in the Window

About ten years after marrying Doug, I'd just completed a yoga teacher training program. I'd found a lovely space above the post office in a small nearby town I could rent by the day as I grew my yoga business. It was a large open room with wooden floors and tall windows. Beautiful. My intention was to grow my business to the point where I could afford to rent the space full-time, which was $800 a month plus utilities. I had *absolutely no doubt* this was the space I was meant to have. So, of course, no prayer was needed. Little did I know what was coming.

When it was time to consider renting full-time, I worked with the rental agent who approached the owner to start negotiations. But there was some delay, as the building had just been sold and the new owner didn't live locally. When the owner was finally contacted, he didn't seem very interested in renting, almost resistant. But I was undeterred! I knew this was my space!

Around that time, one of my sons had come to stay with us. One day, we were walking around our town oval and found ourselves wandering down a short side street. There we paused to look in the window of a small shop being renovated. I said, "Gee, this would make a great little place for a yoga studio—if I were looking for one." It was smaller than the space over the post office, but the location was great and there were no stairs to climb.

The door was open, so my son said, "Let's go in."

An older man painting the walls greeted us warmly. "You all looking for a space?"

My son looked at me. "Maybe," he said.

"Great location," the man said.

"How much?" I heard myself ask.

"$450 a month—everything included."

By this time, he'd stopped painting and was showing us around describing all the renovations he was planning. I felt a quiet resonance with him. Something about what was happening felt easy, effortless . . . like we'd all stepped into some vortex where the scene was already written and we were just playing our parts.

And as natural as could be, I said, "Can I complete an application? I live really close and could get it back to you right away."

"No need. I know you're good," he said reaching out to shake my hand.

"When can I sign the lease?"

"No lease necessary. Just a handshake," he said smiling. And with that, I started a twelve-year relationship as a renter in his building.

But the story wasn't over. Doug and I and our family had recently returned from living in Maine, where we'd owned a large Victorian home. Due to the housing bust in the early 1990s, we weren't able to sell and had to settle for renting. Needing regular maintenance and constant care, this was not the ideal scenario. There'd been one problem after another, and we'd incurred quite a lot of debt. We decided to take all the money I was making in my yoga business and apply it toward paying down the debt, which truly felt insurmountable. In fact, a lawyer friend had suggested we just declare bankruptcy and start over.

But this was right before yoga hit the mainstream, and I was the first and only yoga studio in town. Within two years, I had nine teachers and about two hundred students coming through the door each week. This growth, along with my overhead expenses being roughly half what they'd have been in the space over the post office, enabled us to pay off all our debt within three years!

This is why I often say, "I'm so glad I'm not in charge of my life!" Just another time I absolutely *knew* what was best when, in fact, it was not what God had in mind at all. No. Something infinitely better was waiting just off the town oval, and all it took was a handshake.

Dollars from Heaven

When our youngest daughter was a senior in college, she was anxiously looking forward to her graduation. Unfortunately in late fall she broke her shoulder. This meant she wouldn't be able to continue her part-time job, which was needed to pay for her housing and extracurricular activities. Our agreement with all our kids was that we'd pay for the basic tuition, but they'd need to work to pay for the rest. We felt it was important they had some skin in the game. Panic. We didn't have the extra money for her last semester to get her to graduation. So, off I went to pray.

Shortly after, I was teaching a yoga class when one of my students, Jan, handed me a program, *Mantra: Sacred Words of Power* by Thomas Ashley-Farrand, Namadeva Acharya, a leading authority of Sanskrit mantra.

"Do you know this guy?" she asked. I didn't. "Check it out and let me know what you think."

On the drive home, I put in the first cassette and the very first mantra was "Om Shrim Maha Lakshmiyae Swaha," which the program said was well-known for attracting all forms of abundance, particularly financial abundance. By this time, already in love with mantra, I was on it!

A few weeks later, I was talking with my office administrator, Julie, about creating a different kind of class in the new year—one combining a study of the Bhagavad Gita with yoga practice. I was thinking I'd run it from January through June and offer a night and a day class.

What's important here is that I, initially, was *not* in any way connecting the creation of this new course with the money I was trying to attract for my daughter's tuition. In fact, I remember asking Julie, "Do you think anyone will sign up for this?" It felt like quite a long commitment at the time. But I went ahead and created a flyer and put it out to my yoga students. When people started signing up, the light went on. Within a few weeks, I had an astonishing nineteen students signed up across the night and day classes.

Om Shrim Maha Lakshmiyae Swaha . . .

Soon after, Doug came home and said he'd gotten a bonus at work! Up until that time, he'd *never* gotten a bonus.

Om Shrim Maha Lakshmiyae Swaha . . .

"This is fun!"

Finally, just when I thought it couldn't get any better, a few of my yoga students approached me about creating a mini-retreat. God had sent more than enough financial abundance to cover the extra needed and had left me with an inner smile that continually whispered a joyful . . . *thank you.*

Fun. Magical. Yes.

But nothing compared to the mountain top.

9

The Mountain Top

To Love God Most

You silenced my surest knowing
unarmed my best guess
emptied my will

Pierced my heart and left me bleeding . . . only love . . . for You

I am silent now . . .
sensing only the moist touch of You on my lips

Dying now . . . in sweet ecstasy
Feeling only Your kiss birthing me . . . lifting me . . . onto Your grace

Soaring now . . .
glorious and free

Home to You my Beloved
Home to You.

The climb up the mountain is steep, perilous. It can bloody our knees, excavate and lay bare our most treasured beliefs, and leave our heart silently curled in fetal position, hoping to find its life again. It can leave us alone, disoriented, confused, desperately searching for some—any—familiar, solid ground.

Lucky us. Unhinged and undone, we're now ready for the summit. What we can't know before making the climb is the most blessed of all gifts waits for us there—waits for our unconditional surrender, to leave all behind, falling open and empty, to be filled with only what really matters: the purest and sweetest knowing of all that, regardless of outcomes, we simply love God most, and that's more than enough.

Sometimes a series of events leads us from the valley up toward the summit, and it's only in hindsight we see how perfectly woven they were by God's unseen hand.

"It's Already Rented."

A few years after opening my yoga studio, we bought a small cabin about half an hour from town. One immediate outcome was that my phone bill skyrocketed as I tried to keep up with calls and doing business as usual. This was right before cell phones were the norm. So I decided to find an office in town, ideally somewhere around our town oval, close to my studio. And I'd decided I didn't want to pay more than $250 a month, which was about how much extra I was paying in phone charges.

Doug was working part-time as a real estate agent in an office close to my studio, so I asked him to look around. After searching, he assured me there were no office spaces listed for rent, at least not in the regular multiple listings realtors used.

As I'd already put out my prayer, I just knew there was the perfect office space for me. It was a rainy day when I decided to go to every business around the oval to inquire if there might be something available on the upper floors. I'd come to the last business but still no luck. But as I was thanking the man and leaving, he said, "You may want to try across the street at the Stickney Building. There're some offices upstairs."

"Great. Thank you. I will."

The Stickney Building was right next to the real estate agency where my husband was working, and I did already know of several businesses on the second floor. But last I'd heard, all the offices had been rented for quite a while. But, as my last resort, I climbed up to the second floor and then noticed the middle office on the right was empty. I asked someone across the hall about it, and they said the tenants had just moved out.

"Who owns this building?" I asked.

"Dick at Dick's Barber Shop downstairs."

"Oh, okay. Thanks."

So, down I went to the barber shop. Dick was busy cutting hair.

"Hi," I said introducing myself. "I own the Tree of Life Yoga Studio over on Middle Street. I'm interested in your vacant room upstairs to use as an office. I see you're busy. I'll leave my card here on the shelf. Please call me when you can."

"It's already rented," he said without looking at me. "I showed it this morning, and I think the people are going to take it."

"Oh, okay. But if it doesn't work out with them, I hope you'll give me a call." I left my card on a shelf and walked out. I actually thought he'd been borderline rude. A couple of weeks went by and no word. Then, the message came on my answering machine:

"Stephanie, this is Dick the barber. Sorry I haven't gotten back to you. I've had the flu. Anyway, if you're still interested in the room upstairs, I'll rent it to you. I do have to charge $150 a month, but that's everything included. Give me a call if you're still interested."

It was perfect, of course. Less than I'd hoped and close to my yoga studio. But more importantly, it was the beginning of a deeply spiritual journey with Dick the barber and a beloved Mother Teresa rosary.

Lost and Found

For reasons I can't explain, I've always had a deep affinity for Mother Teresa of Calcutta, now Saint Teresa, and, while I've had no experience with the Catholic Church, her life has been a guiding inspiration. Once when visiting the Chimayo mission in New Mexico, I'd bought a rosary solely because it had her picture on it, and I'd become fond of calling it my Mother Teresa rosary. Every morning, I'd use it for my Mantra Prayers instead of a traditional *mala*. It was *never* far from me.

One morning, I went to retrieve it from my prayer bowl and it wasn't there. Instantly, I remembered it'd been on my lap in the car the day before, and I guessed it'd probably fallen out during one of my stops. I drove into town and retraced all of my steps. I checked around each spot where I'd parked and up and down the sidewalks. No rosary. I tried praying for many days, fervently. Still, no rosary.

Finally, I accepted it wasn't going to return. As I could see no reason why that particular object would go missing, I truly felt, somehow, for some reason, it must have been needed elsewhere. I told myself I'd get another one during our next trip to the Chimayo mission.

And life went on.

A short time later, I ran into Dick. He told me about his daughter, who'd come into some very difficult times with her health and her job. He was very worried about her.

And life went on.

Then, one day in the spring, Dick came up to my office to check the air conditioner. As we talked, he noticed the Mother Teresa tapestry hanging on the wall above my desk.

He said, "You know, just before the holidays, a woman brought a rosary into my shop she'd found in the snow outside. It had a picture of Mother Teresa on it." Instantly, I started jumping up and down hugging him! I scarcely noticed the blank stare on his face.

"I called everyone I knew, but I didn't call you because I didn't think you were Catholic. But do you remember my daughter? Well, I'm not a praying man, but I do believe in God. So, I decided to pray for my daughter with the rosary. Since then, her health has miraculously improved and she's gotten a new job."

He paused a moment and then said, "See, you lost it because I needed it and now it's time for you to have it back."

"We Put You In"

I rented the office in the Stickney Building from Dick for a few years before moving into the larger space, where the antique store had been, which had a room for an office. Then later, I moved my yoga studio to a nearby town. By then I was calling it the Tree of Life School for Sacred Living to reflect my shift to ministry. Since moving, I'd rarely seen Dick, except to wave through the barbershop window when, occasionally, I'd walk by. But Doug got his hair cut there once a month, so we kept in touch that way.

One day, shortly after moving to the nearby town, I was about to start a daylong class in the seminary program I'd created. About half an hour before everyone was to arrive, I felt a strange sensation. I went to the bathroom and saw I was bleeding. Being five years postmenopausal, I knew that wasn't good. After making a quick run to the store, I walked back into my space and looked up at my Mother Teresa tapestry hanging on the wall. I remembered how she'd carried on, fully committed to her mission, regardless of what was happening in her life. I would do the same, and we went on to have a beautiful day.

The next morning, I made an appointment with my doctor and went out for some errands. When I returned home, Doug said there was a message on our answering machine from Dick the barber. He'd never called me before. In the message, he said he and his wife had returned from Chimayo, and he'd brought me something. He asked if I'd stop by the barbershop sometime to pick it up. Then he said, "I love you. God bless you." Now, although we certainly had a special connection due to the former experience with my Mother Teresa Rosary, he'd never spoken to me like that. I remember feeling struck—something important was happening.

Meanwhile, my doctor had told me I needed to see a gynecologist to rule out uterine cancer, and a few days later I had an appointment for an ultrasound. The nurse practitioner said I had a thickening of the uterine wall and a polyp. She wasn't concerned about the polyp but said I needed to return as soon as possible to see the gynecologist and have a biopsy taken of the uterine wall.

After my appointment, I went by the barbershop to see Dick. He was busy but handed me a Mother Teresa rosary with hearts on it he'd brought back from Chimayo. I thanked him fiercely and turned to leave, but as I did, I clearly heard him say in the ethers, "Don't worry. We've got you covered. We put you in." Now Chimayo is known for many healings, as the dirt in one section of the chapel floor has a long history of curative powers. There're crutches on the walls, notes, medicine bottles. I knew, in that moment, I was in trouble and, also, I was going to be okay—regardless of the outcome. And, of course, Dick could have had no way of knowing, consciously, what was going on with me.

The day after I'd seen the bleeding, I'd started a healing practice using an ancient Vedic mantra of Shiva, the Maha Mrityunjaya Mantra, well-known for its healing properties. Each time I chanted the mantra, I held my Mother Teresa rosary against my belly and thanked her, Jesus, and Shiva for healing where there was any disease. I fell asleep each night and awoke each morning chanting with my rosary on my belly. Throughout the day, I played a beautiful instrumental of "Amazing Grace," as I just knew some grace was surely being played out in my life.

And I started to feel deeply—sweetly—that although I certainly didn't want to be seriously ill, what I wanted most was what my God wanted for me, and I started ending my prayers with, "I belong to you. Always have. I love you most, so, whatever you want for me is fine." This tender awareness turned out to be *the* most blessed gift of this experience and continues to restore peace to my heart every time I find myself in any kind of trouble. *I love you most, God. I love you most.* It is always and forever enough.

When I returned for the biopsy, I felt oddly calm. After the nurses had prepped me, the gynecologist came in looking quite serious and focused. Then, as she looked closely at the screen, her expression changed. Looking relieved she said, "Okay, this is good. I'm happy and happy for you. When I looked at your ultrasound last week I was concerned and, coming in here, I thought this is not going to be good. But, now, your uterine wall looks thin and perfectly healthy. We should get that polyp out, and we'll send it for a biopsy, but it doesn't look like anything to be concerned about."

And, indeed, all was well. Amen.

Later, I wrote this story and shared it with her and Dick.

A Blessing from Medjugorje

I wore it for a long time, until it finally withered off my wrist. It'd come on my birthday in a small box from my lifelong friend Jane, far away, the same one who'd come to stay with me when Dean left. I was surprised because, though we exchanged cards and sometimes a phone call on our birthdays, we hadn't exchanged gifts in many years. Yet, when I opened the box, I understood. It was a *Breathe Blessing* bracelet, and the packaging said, "Made with love in the small pilgrimage town of Medjugorje." Medjugorje is, of course, where Mother Mary has appeared since 1981, giving messages to the world. My dear friend had absolutely no idea what had been happening in my life. Later, she would tell me she just knew she'd been drawn to send it to me. You'll understand the significance of this gift by the end of this story—a story that has left me *gratia plena*, full of grace.

After an extremely busy year, I was looking forward to my summer break and my hammock. What I didn't realize was how much my body was needing the rest, for by the first week of June, I started having neck and head pain. During that time, a church member had dropped by to pick up the key to our sanctuary, as I was too sick to go in for a meeting. In our brief conversation, he'd told Doug and me he'd recently had Bell's palsy. But in my state, the story barely registered.

Within a few days, I woke and noticed my mouth felt strange. I looked in the mirror and saw that one side was drooping and not responsive to any of my efforts to fix it. Doug immediately took me to the ER. My mother had had her first stroke at about my age at the time. I remember feeling numb. After a brief examination, the doctor said quite matter-of-factly, "It looks like you've had a stroke in the middle of the night. We'll get a CT scan to be sure. Meanwhile, I'm going to admit you." And, off he went. *What? Is this really happening?* my heart wailed.

After two CT scans and an MRI came back normal, the doctor was clearly puzzled. By this time, one of my daughters had arrived and noticed my right eye was not closing in sync with my left. Somehow this cued the doctor to take another look. "Okay, now I understand. It's Bell's palsy."

"So, no stroke?" I asked. "And, what is Bell's palsy?" not recalling the earlier conversation with my church friend. After some explanation, I was released with medication. Feeling numb, all that kept repeating in my head was *what just happened?*

Shortly after returning home, I wrote to my community asking for prayers. That evening one of my dear friends, to whom I'd loaned my Mother Teresa rosary, called to insist she come over and return it. At some point, she suggested we pray together stressing, "The rosary, you know, is really all about Mother Mary."

At that moment, it struck me that, for all my extraordinary experiences with the rosary, not being a Catholic, I'd always associated my rosary with Mother Teresa. But on that night, and on every day and night that followed, I held my rosary close and started calling on Mother Mary and soon could feel her presence very near to me.

A few days later, I went to see my doctor for the follow-up visit.

"The doctor at the hospital ordered a test for Lyme," he said. "The first results have come back positive. We're going to send it off for the next level to verify. I'll call you in a few days to let you know." Feeling better and still elated not to have had a stroke, I thought, *hummmm, Lyme? Okay. I can handle that*, and was impatient to leave.

Then I noticed a slight shift in his posture as he looked down at my chart. A pause.

"But there's something else we need to talk about. One of the CT scans taken at the hospital shows a spot on your lungs, a small nodule. It looks like the kind that can grow unnoticed and stay silent for years until finally lung cancer is diagnosed, but by then it's often too late." Looking up at me, he said, "If this is the case, we can say, 'Thank you, Bell's palsy!'"

What? Geeeeeees!! What else??? I screamed silently.

"The hospital will call you in the next few days to schedule another CT scan. Try not to worry. We're just trying to be sure."

On the ride home, it suddenly became very clear why Mother Mary felt very near to me. I told Doug but decided not to say anything to anyone else until I knew for sure. But right away, I was drawn to write a prayer and send love to my nodule. Gently touching my upper lungs . . .

"Little one, what has formed you? What are you here to tell me? I am listening. Help me to receive all you have for me. Talk to me in the silence so we may be healed. Meanwhile, know I am infusing you with love. Be well, little one, for all is well."

I started saying this prayer all during the day—in the shower, in the car, in my hammock. I began and ended each day with my rosary thanking Mother Mary, Mother Teresa, and Jesus for being with me, for holding me in their tender care and healing love. And, blessedly, my nodule silently spoke to me in quiet moments, letting me know the feelings it held, its deeper message, and gifting me with what changes needed to come.

The next week, I had my CT scan, and a few days later, right before my birthday, the doctor called to tell me, quite happily, that the nodule was gone. In fact, no irregular tissues were found.

Recall now the beginning of this story: receiving the *Breathe Blessing* bracelet from my friend Jane that had been made in the small pilgrimage town of Medjugorje. For me, this confirmed what I'd felt all along—Mother Mary had been with me, was with me, and, as importantly, would continue to be with me going forward.

I believe there are times when we can be cured of our ailments, but true healing only comes with love . . . the kind I believe Mother Mary helped me send to my nodule . . . the kind that in the end knows that regardless of the outcome, we're going to be okay because we already have, pulsing in our veins and steadily beating our hearts, the greatest love of all. And, in the remembering, I am left . . . *Gratia plena.*

Amen.

PART V

Surprise and Delight

10

When God Smiles

Where I Might Not Have Thought to Look

You paused me

And I'm left fluttering aloft . . .
like one of those hummingbirds outside my window
waiting with only the sweet scent of You holding me

suspended . . .
full of Your wonder.

I love it when God smiles, turning my heart inside out, surprising, startling me when and where I least expected it. It reminds me again and again where the mystery lies—just beyond my wildest imaginings.

Five Dollars

It was a bright, breezy afternoon, and I was driving on a busy city street with the windows down and music blaring. And then came to a red light. I was first in line.

Suddenly, there he was. One of those homeless men I'd seen many times, the ones who carry signs. Now, I'm quite certain that only by the grace of God have I never been homeless. Still, I struggle with what to do when approached on the street in this way. It's that awful mix of wanting to help but wondering if my help could only make things worse. So, I sat there, my mind racing: *Quick! Look away! Roll up the window! Light, change!!*

But, still, he kept coming and once he was at my door, I slowly looked up at him. And I was paused. In that moment, and it was just an instant, I fully understood what Mother Teresa meant when she'd said, "We look but we don't *see*," because in that moment, I *saw* him—or, rather he *saw* me—or both? No words. I simply took out my wallet and gave him the first bill I found, $5. He smiled kindly, the light changed, and off I went.

An instant I can't fully explain, yet one that lives on in me all these years later. Sometimes when remembering, I get a flash of him on the school bus on the first day of school. I can see him learning to ride a bike, wobbling back and forth down the street, determined. I picture him a bit awkward and clumsy around his first love. I wonder if he'd played a sport, had a hobby. What was home like? And, mostly, what dreams had collapsed bringing him to the curb that day?

And I've wondered if our brief exchange was soon forgotten, our glance a hiccup before moving on to the next car, and what possible dent my $5 could have made in his heavy load.

We look but we don't see.

Mostly, my heart shutters a bit, thinking of how egregiously unequal our exchange was. He gave me the blessed opportunity to *see* him: a walking, breathing, struggling, kindred soul in this messy thing we call life. And for me, too, to feel *seen*. All I was able to give in return was $5.

Wherever you are, dear brother, thank you.

Open Letter to the Man on the Sidewalk

Have you thought about it since? You were so mad at me because you thought I was laughing at you. That day my husband and I passed you on the sidewalk downtown. You were packing up when you and I, by chance, caught a glance.

"What are you laughing at—you piece of white . . . shit!"

My knee-jerk reaction got stuck on the first line. I wanted to say, *No! I wasn't laughing at you!* I'm sure I've hurt people in many ways, but laughing at someone is not one of them. If you knew me, you'd know why. Still, I'm truly sorry you took it that way. But it was the second part that caught my breath—said with that rage-hot look you gave me. It's why we kept walking.

I've thought a lot about that look. You see, I recognized it because I've seen it in my own family. It's all too familiar—most often caused by the malicious, debilitating festering of addiction. Yes, I'm a mother who knows the unspeakable heartbreak caused by the malignant suffering hidden behind that look.

Still, I'm not excusing you for what you did. It was *not* okay to verbally attack me, someone you just happened to make eye contact with. No, not okay. And in case you think I'm one of those White, hippie, granola, "Kumbaya" types, writing with some assumption that it could all be made better if we could just sit together, you'd be wrong. That would be a whitewash (forgive the expression) over the moment, wouldn't it?

No, I realize the bridge across racial and economic divides is narrow and frail and won't hold anyone not ready or unable to take full responsibility for everyone's safe passage. It's hard work. It requires uneasy listening and true hearing. No, sitting here in my comfortable surroundings, I wouldn't presume to know what you've known. What brought you to the sidewalk that day. What deep struggles keep you desperately searching for what will numb it all away. What you've seen, experienced. I wouldn't presume to know . . . but wish I could.

I'm not sure why you were put on my path that day, but I want you to know I know it wasn't *you* who taunted me but rather it was the unabating rage, desperation, and spewing out of addiction. And I want you to know, behind that look I do fully recognize *you,* my brother, a fellow human being, like me.

I pray God's grace will somehow deliver this note to you, and one day you'll find your way out from behind that look. If so, maybe then, you'll remember the day when an older White woman, passing by, glanced at you, smiling.

And, perhaps, perhaps then . . . we could meet on that narrow bridge.

America Runs on Delight!

For a longtime we didn't know her name. We just knew every Friday morning we'd get to hear *that* voice: "Good morning! Welcome to Dunkin' Donuts. May I take your order?" Doug and I, making our weekly drive to watch our grandbaby, would always stop at that same Dunkin' Donuts for breakfast. And over time, we got to be regulars.

"Hey guys! How ya doin'?" she'd say as she handed us our coffee and sandwiches. Then one day, I asked offhandedly, "What's your name?"

"Julie," she said.

"Thank you, Julie."

And so, from then on, we got to thank her personally. And each time we'd leave smiling. It always made me chuckle how good I felt driving away with those sandwiches.

Then, one Friday, a strange voice. "Well, she'll probably be at the window." But she wasn't. "Gee, hope she's not sick. Maybe she's off today. Sure hope we get to see her next week." But we didn't. And not the next week either. Finally, we had to admit our sweet dose of Friday morning delight was gone forever from our lives. Would seem like such a small thing. It wasn't.

In the weeks following, I found myself wondering what it was that made those short encounters so special. After all, we knew nothing about her. And each encounter was the same ol' rote dialogue in replay. Yet it seemed it didn't matter. In those few short seconds, she'd made us feel like she had all the time in the world for us—like something a little special was going on right there at that drive-through.

Surprisingly, it didn't seem important to know the usual things. No long conversations or intimate understanding required. No detailed knowledge of her history, her struggles, or dreams needed. No. It seemed her simple presence, infused into the mundane ritual of the fast-food drive-by, was quite enough—enough to make those moments come alive and to leave a sweet fragrance lingering, now, over a lifetime.

Sometimes I've imagined a whole new ad campaign for the fast-food giant. I've pictured large billboards all over the country with Julie's face scattering, with unbridled ease, that smile of hers on all those unsuspecting passengers. And just below her picture would be the new slogan: *America Runs on Delight!*

Pelican Bay State Prison

Late one afternoon, I stepped out to check the mail in front of my yoga studio. There I found a letter addressed to me from an inmate I'll call John Smith in the Security Housing Unit of Pelican Bay State Prison. Thinking it must be a mistake, I almost put it back to be returned to sender. Then, cautiously, I opened it. I found four handwritten pages that still pause my heart and leave it silent. My first book, *An Ordinary Life Transformed: Lessons for Everyone from the Bhagavad Gita*, had come out about six months before and, through a series of what can only be described as divinely orchestrated events, John had gotten a copy. Here are excerpts from his letter:

> I am a 39-year-old inmate who, since 1992, have been serving a life without the possibility of parole prison sentence. It may appear strange to you, but I am isolated from all human contact. When I leave my cell, it is always under escort while being handcuffed, and I am allowed only ninety minutes a day outside alone in a tiny cage. Rev. Stephanie Rutt I have read your book quite a few times and I am writing to say thank you for being a light in my journey. For if it was not for your book I would not be where I am beginning at now . . . I have a long way to go . . . but I feel freer than I've ever been in my life, that I can truly remember. I lived in the real world as a prisoner and most of my prison sentence as one also, but I am slowly freeing myself, and beginning to spread my wings . . . I am sure you never would have thought that you could reach through concrete and steel and touch someone's life. But better yet I believe this is exactly why you wrote this book and presented it as a gift to the world. So that one day all of us could feel the true meaning of "Welcome Home."

What John couldn't have known is I'd often used his very words to describe my book—*my gift to God and to the world*. I did write back to thank him for his letter, but never heard from him again. I've shared his letter with my community many times as an example of what can happen, what's possible, when we simply do what we can where we are, and offer our small part to the greater tapestry of life. What can happen when we don't concern ourselves with where God's unseen hand may lead or what effect our humble offerings may have. What's possible when we remember our only job is to show up, offer what we're able to in faith and love, and trust that God will do the rest. How freeing . . . for us, and most especially, in this case, for John.

Welcome Home, John . . . Welcome Home.

11

Fairies in Disguise

The Little People

Stare softly, You winked
see me

sparkling . . . everywhere
hidden just behind

Listen closely, You whispered
hear me

silent . . . in that space
between words

Beware when the little ones show up! Disclaimer! You just may come unraveled.

Under the Weeping Willow

Pigtails. Bright smile. Bridging childhood and the coming moon time. My heart reaches back to a memory of her, maybe three years old making her way, not so carefully, down the side steps of our cabin. Yellow polka dot dress with matching frilly cap. But it's the eyes I remember most. Clear, focused, peering out, revealing a glimpse of the aged crown silent within, already knowing where her small body should go.

My first grandchild. The one I'd see much less often, as she lived far away from the grandchildren to come who'd live close by. Still, maybe it was the short visits that made them all the more sweet. Our favorite thing was to have tea parties. My knees squeezed tight under the small table as I prayed the tiny chair would hold up. But my granddaughter would be way too busy pouring our delectable tea, giggling, brimming over with chin-up girly confidence, to notice any awkwardness in her special guest. No, I'm quite certain no 5-Star restaurant could have ever left me feeling more pampered.

One Christmas I gave her a tea set that had a design of roses on it. It was one of those that comes packaged in tight plastic. But it was special to me, as it'd reminded me of the dishes my grandmother had placed safe in the china cabinet, the ones we only used on special occasions. Somehow, I just knew, or hoped, she'd feel that same special feeling when she got them from across the miles. Such are the flights of fancy of a yearning heart.

But on this day, pigtails, lanky legs, budding beauty. It was Thanksgiving at our new home, and we were blessed to have the family gather. A special treat. As we gathered around the table, holding hands, each offered some words, thoughts, for the moment. I remember my dear granddaughter, with a sure, clear, voice led us all in a prayer, spoken straight from her love of Jesus. I couldn't help smiling, proud to witness her being so brave and true. A soon-to-be woman I knew would lead any and all blessed to land in her sphere.

Still, the most poignant memory would happen under the weeping willow cherry tree in our front yard, our last tea party. Perfect, actually, for a new day. This time, we both had to squeeze low under the long hanging limbs to crawl in and set up our make-shift dishes. And we also snuck in some treats. *Shhhhh! Our secret!*

"So, what kind of tea shall we have today?" I don't remember how long we lingered for the time paused as my heart opened tenderly to hold the short time in forever. A forever that graciously returns every time I close my eyes and remember.

Now a grown beautiful woman training to be a minister, just like the one who first appeared all those years ago at our Thanksgiving table. A servant of the Holy Spirit, a scholar of the Word, forging her path daring to use her own voice in her own way to witness as only the Lord directs.

And me, I stand holding fast to a yellow polka-dot dress with matching frilly cap, a rose-covered tea set, and a memory of that last tea part under the weeping willow. And in the dreamtime, I hear . . .

"What kind of tea shall we have today?"

"Uh, how about the one that'll last forever?"

"Okay," she said, eyes smiling.

And so, it has.

A Modern-Day Shepherd Boy

Truly, had I not witnessed it myself, I would've never believed it. It actually started four years before when my oldest grandson, who has autism, was nine years old. At the time, I was immersed in Psalm 23 in Hebrew, as I mentioned in *Half a Second*, and one day was playing a recording. Right away he took to it so I recited it with him a couple of times, and then he was off to do other things.

A week later, without hearing the recording, he simply starting reciting the full psalm again. While some of the words were slightly slurred, anyone familiar with the psalm in Hebrew would have instantly recognized it. I was astonished! And in the weeks that followed, he continued to just say the psalm again and again for what seemed to be his own pleasure.

Now, fast forward four years. My grandson, my son, Doug and I were sitting around the dinner table talking about some of the speeches and passages my grandson was being asked to learn and memorize in school. Suddenly, I had the urge to ask, "Do you remember when you could say the 23rd Psalm in Hebrew?

"Yes," my grandson answered with great confidence.

"*Adonai roee lo echsar. . .*" I said to help him get started. But he quickly stopped me.

"No, Grandma."

Then, he sat up a little taller and recited the full psalm in Hebrew without error! I'm still amazed when I think about it!

Now, I'm aware that those having knowledge of autism might suggest such instances are within the behavioral spectrum. True. But I consider it a kind of miracle that a young boy, largely non-verbal except for short directive sentences, could hear Psalm 23 only a few times, in a language not his own, and then be able to recite it without effort or practice four years later.

There *is* something inherently intrinsic, even captivating, about the Hebrew language. Similar to Aramaic, Sanskrit, and Arabic, for example, each letter has its own essence and purpose and seems to hold close its song reserved only for those ready to sing aloud. When the letters are strung together into words, the soul seems to effortlessly recognize itself and becomes a kind of songbird involuntarily quivering to the sweet harmonies of the creator. My grandson did not *learn* Psalm 23. He simply listened once or twice and then, without effort, became an instrument for the sound of God. And for those of us blessed to hear . . . well, we were left in wonder and awe.

Now, especially each year as Jews around the world celebrate Hanukkah, the Festival of Lights, I pause to remember the miracle of light that shone though my grandson's strong and certain voice as he, a young shepherd boy of today, found resonance with the Mizor L'David, the Psalm of David, and with the shepherd boy of long ago who would become a great king.

I am fully certain they walk together in this valley of the shadow of death. And, I trust they will continue to be followed by goodness and mercy and dwell in the house of the Lord forever.

A Kiddy Bowl and a Grown-Up Spoon

One afternoon, shortly after Easter, I'd gotten my youngest grand-daughter, then five years old, off the bus, and we were relaxing at her kitchen table enjoying a snack. Suddenly, she quite excitedly started telling me about going to a *very* big, *really* beautiful church where she saw this man in a long robe bless the Easter food by sprinkling water on it. Her other grandparents are Catholic and on occasion would bring her to special services. I responded by saying how wonderful it must have been and just let the moment be full with the memory.

Then, a little later, I said casually, "You know how when you come to our house for a meal and we go around the table saying a prayer and then we thank the animal for its life, for the meat we're about to eat?"

"Yeah," she said, squinting a bit.

"Well, I think of that as a kind of blessing. So, any time you want to remember how thankful you are for all the great food you have, you can offer a blessing too. Fold your hands like this and say something like, 'Thank you God for all this good food I'm about to eat, and thank you chicken, or whatever the animal is, for your life so I can grow big and strong.'"

A pause and I could see the wheels churning, "You mean *I* can bless the food?"

"Of course," I answered.

And before I knew it, she jumped up and pointed with strong resolve to the cupboard where her and her younger brother's dishes were kept.

"Quick, Grandma! Get a bowl and put some water in it and get me a spoon—a big grown-up spoon."

Dutifully I did as I was ordered, as I could sense something quite special was swirling around in that heart of hers. I filled a small plastic bowl, one with a suction bottom, half full of water and placed it with a large wooden spoon on the table in front of her. Meanwhile, she ran to get the Polish pastries she said that she and her dad had made the night before but "hadn't tasted so good."

Then, seating herself in front of the bowl and spoon, she paused, folded her hands, closed her eyes, and prayed, "Please God, bless this food so it will taste good by tomorrow. My daddy and I really tried to make it good but it didn't work." She then took the spoon and half flung, half dripped, water over the pastries.

"There," she said, quite satisfied, "I'm sure they'll taste good by tomorrow."

Yikes! I thought. *Now, what'll I do?* Besides, I reasoned, the pastries *could* taste better by tomorrow, right? Miracles do happen!

Finally, I arrived on something I thought might save her heartfelt blessing. I said, "Well, honey, I don't know if they'll taste better by tomorrow, but your blessing was very sweet and, you know, I think you and your daddy making something together was probably the biggest blessing."

Woops! Furled brow!

"No, Grandma! I blessed the food. I *know* it will taste better by tomorrow!"

"Okay, honey. I'm quite sure you're right."

"Grandma, let's play now!" Blessing time was over.

I didn't see my granddaughter again until the following week, and in the annals of a five-year-old's memory, that's a lifetime, so I never did ask if the pastries had indeed tasted better the next day. Instead, I chose to believe simply that one of those unexplained miracles had most surely happened and to hold fast to what I felt had been the true blessing of that afternoon . . .

One of God's beloved children had learned that, with a heart-felt prayer, she, too, could bless what she felt was most in need of blessing in her small world. No, it wasn't in a big beautiful church. And it wasn't offered by a person wearing a long robe, sprinkling holy water from a chalice. It was at a modest kitchen table offered by a five-year-old's praying hands, and all that was needed was a small plastic kiddy bowl, half-filled with it-must-be-holy water from the tap and, oh yes, a grown-up spoon.

I do believe it was . . . God's true blessing.

Guru "One Sock"

I'd nicknamed my youngest grandson "One Sock," as it seemed he was always losing one of them. But one day, when he was three years old, he became my guru on one of our treasure hunts out in that wild, wondrous backyard of his.

Knowing full well the time to embark, he'd always point to the yard in captain style saying, "Treasyour! Treasyour!" and, with his Thomas the Engine treasure box close in hand, would push open the screen door. No time to waste! Off we'd go!

Soon, he'd pause to pick up a small piece of bark. "Treasyour, Gamah," and it'd go right into his box. A few steps later, he'd hold up a small leaf. "Treasyour. Treasyour!" And, over a short period of time, his little treasure box would become quite full.

One day, I saw what looked like a true treasure, a white crystal. "Treasure, One Sock!" I said, "Treasure!" as I bent low to hold it close, imagining a kind of teaching moment about this special treasure. But my grandson seemed neither impressed nor deterred. Slowly, he guided me along and then paused to pick up one of those quite ordinary treasures camouflaged among all the other nondescript rocks. "Treasyour, Gamah. Treasyour." And then cheese crackers, a fruit cup, and naptime called and our treasure hunt ended.

Now, I'll leave it to others to debate what was or was not musing in the mind of my grandson that day and what may or may not most accurately be called a treasure. But for me, in the quiet of the afternoon, I found myself contemplating the true treasure I'd been led to discover. And, I heard the voice of the Holy One . . .

"Pause. Here I am waiting to be known in the very places you may least suspect. Remember. I bring forth all creation and delight in all My expressions. There is no hierarchy or grades of importance in My holiness. There is no part of My creation more beloved by Me than another. It's easy to forget this when you see something you think is special but, truly, I'm equally present in what you may think is only ordinary. When you learn this, you'll see Me everywhere. And, like One Sock, you'll delight in everything."

Thank you, One Sock.

PART VI

Wild and Free

12

Hidden Wonder

The Soul of the World

Shhhhhhh . . .
Listen only with your heart

The rolling rocks, soft green moss, and the circling eagle are singing . . .
singing just for you.

A love song from a distant star

In *Eagle's Gift*, I described how the Spirit of the Eagle had helped me to accept the changes that were coming to our special place, the one Doug and I had discovered many years ago in the wilds of Maine. These stories take you back to the beginning to come full circle.

Only here do I discover how few clothes I need, that my hair tie is a most sacred object, and a thank you to the fish for its life is the true blessing. It's where I started my spiritual journey and where now, in the twilight of life, I'm drawn to return more and more—to the Soul of the World where perfect silence speaks of all there is.

The Wild Inner Sacred

You would've never found it unless you knew just where to look. The old logging road was grown up, and the waterway entry was stealthily guarded by rocky boulders. But such is the way when in search of the sacred. Lucky for us, we stumbled upon it some thirty-five years ago—this sacred piece of wilderness, at the end of forty miles of dirt roads into the Maine forest, Doug and I would come to call *our* special place.

At the time, I can't say we were in search of the sacred. No, it was much more like a desperate need to escape the bugs. Doug had convinced me to try wilderness camping, a far cry for me, a city girl, who'd never even been to a campground. But he was so enthusiastic and kept insisting over and over, without a doubt, it was going to be wonderful. I wasn't so sure, but his insistence carried the day. So, off we went in search of that dream wilderness campsite somewhere hidden deep in the Maine woods.

Right at dusk, we arrived at the end of a dirt road surrounded by dense, ominous woods. Doug, trying to read the map by flashlight, said he thought the wilderness campsite should be close by. *Thought??* I hadn't gotten that far yet, as I was still trying to figure out how we were going to escape the swarm of mosquitoes now circling our car—arriving, I was sure, with great amazement that such a ripe delectable feast had been so graciously laid out before them—us.

Soon we noticed what looked like a path heading straight into those dense woods. But with darkness looming, we had no choice. In we went. After some distance, we saw the remains of a campsite, just up from a stream, long cold. Doug rushed to make a fire, and we set up our tent. As night settled around us, he kept fanning the smoke my way (sweet guy that he is) to deter the thick veil of bugs now eagerly feasting. I was not smiling.

I don't remember much about that first night, but the next morning we decided to hike up the densely covered path. Soon we noticed a very narrow opening that looked like it led through some tall bushes. Curious, we followed. Within just a few feet we emerged out onto a wide-open knoll. Perched high, we found ourselves looking out over a lake on one side, a beautiful pond leading down to a stream on the other, and we heard a kind of waterfall caused by a downed bridge from years past. I'm not sure we took in all the natural beauty at first. Mainly, we were just relieved to feel a cool breeze and, finally, not to be swatting the bugs.

But, no doubt, heaven had arrived.

For many years we returned to canoe, bathe, and frolic in the pond, where we got to know the large turtle whose Spirit guarded and blessed our entrance. And we were thrilled to see all the flegling pines around the edges of our knoll grow taller and taller each year reaching up with green gladness toward the sun. They became our friends, guides and keepers of this sacred place.

I've often reflected upon how the discovery of the outer wild places does mirror our inner wild places, the places we soon encounter as we approach the adventure of our spiritual walk and practice. Sometimes we begin with great excitement. This is going to be great! Finally, I'm going to find peace! (and the Great Spirit smiles compassionately) Other times we may feel called but are a bit hesitant. We may be anxious about being pulled out of our comfort zone and settling into the ominous woods of our inner territory. It's dark in there! What'll I find? And, of course, our first encounter is the mosquito pit, which we came to affectionately call the first site we'd found, representing those impinging fears, the cloaked emotions hidden well in the light of day, and all those pesky aches and pains. Yikes! This is not what I thought!

But as I've discovered again and again, if I persevere, go even deeper, the Great Spirit will lay before me a narrow opening inviting—no, compelling—me into a love, a beauty I've yet to know.

And my Spirit sings.

Don't Tell Heaven

Let this be our special secret for I'm quite certain I've found the *real* heaven right here on earth. You see, I've seen stars glistening over the rippled waters as shades of blue play and fade into green and earthen brown on the rocky shores close by. I've met the Spirit of the Turtle who guards the pond where I've submerged to reemerge again and again. I've felt the shelter of the deep dome of sky with its airy clouds, as the Spirit of the Wind whispers a slight chill of the change to come. No, this is not the land of milk and honey. It *is* a land as lush and pristine as it is untamed and raw. I've learned to walk with sure footing and clear eyes through this heaven's gate, for its landing is at once soft *and* thorny.

The Spirit of this place thrives on its own terms. It awakens in me some deep slumber scabbed over by multitasking, over-scheduling, and the bombardment of a world escalating in chaos. Within this heaven's gate, I am stripped down, made simple and, on a bed of pine straw, sacrificed to the Spirit of the Wild. And as the wood gives its life to the fire, I too release into the scent of smoke all I carry that keeps my soul ladened, hobbling, and worn.

Yes, don't tell heaven it's not heaven. But tell all who may hear that heaven is near, alive, and beckoning all around us. Leave the familiar sidewalks. Escape the known way. Follow the silent call of the trail, once defined by footprints, now hiding beneath wispy ferns, dried limbs, soft mosses, dugout pits, wayward grasses, deserted stumps and wispy wild flowers.

Follow. It will take you deep into places unknown where heaven's gate will open wide to welcome you . . . hone you . . . and, perhaps, at long last, birth you . . .

Wild and free.

Deliverance!

Sometimes the funniest things happen in the wilderness! When Doug and I were visiting our special spot, we could often go a whole week without seeing a soul. We were so isolated it wasn't a spot others might happen upon. Until one fateful day.

We'd been there about five days, so we were very, shall we say, backwoods-ripe. Doug's shirt and shorts were covered with blood from cleaning fish every day. Mine were covered with days of mud, dirt, and food stains. Our bodies were fairly clean, as we'd swim and bathe in the pond every day. But by this time, I could imagine we both looked very foreboding, even scary, to an unsuspecting visitor.

But soon it would get even scarier! I'd recently started taking workshops in shamanism, and Doug asked if I'd do a journey to get information about a special object, a rabbit's foot his grandfather had left him when he'd passed. Doug had been serving overseas at the time and hadn't been able to come home for the funeral. Receiving the rabbit's foot was special to him, as he'd always felt very close to his grandfather. To help me journey to find out what I could, he offered to drum for me.

Now, in order to travel undisturbed to the other realms, I needed to get inside one of our sleeping bags and put a mosquito net over my head. That way there'd be no pesky distractions from our wilderness crawlers or flying friends.

Doug sat close, cross-legged in his bloodstained shirt and shorts, wearing a stained red ball cap tilted sideways and touting five good days of beard growth. The bloodstained knife he'd used to clean fish for our midday meal was laying close by. He started drumming and off I went to the other realms.

But soon, we heard voices. Doug got up and saw two men wearing crispy shirts, wondering into our camp.

"Hello," I heard Doug say trying to be welcoming. But they were already quickly retreating back to their kayaks saying something offhandedly about being from a college in Boston and just looking for the start of the Machias River. By the time I'd gotten out of the sleeping bag, our two visitors had escaped, and Doug was standing there looking very perplexed.

"They sure took off pretty quick," he said. And then we both burst out laughing as we suddenly realized the scene they'd happened upon: a man with a bloodstained shirt and shorts beating a drum, a bloodstained knife close by, and a body, seemingly lifeless, fully shrouded in a sleeping bag!

As for the rabbit's foot, I'd do another journey and see how Doug's grandfather had carried the rabbit's foot, one of his few possessions, with him when he'd come to this country from Ireland, hoping it'd bring him good luck in the new world.

It had. He'd lived a long and good life. Shortly after Doug's grandmother had passed, his wife of over fifty years, he'd painted the window boxes where she'd always loved to plant flowers and then laid down and died a peaceful death. Now it was Doug's turn to receive the rabbit foot's good luck.

And meanwhile, I imagine, still echoing down the halls of academia somewhere in Boston, is a story being told by two professors of how one day they happened upon their own version of the movie *Deliverance* deep in the wilds of Maine!

Singing the Soul of the World

For many summers I'd written about our favorite spot in the Maine wilderness, and every year I'd rejoiced in what we'd received. Our last visit was different—yet equally wonderful, perhaps even more so, in a way I couldn't have anticipated.

This time, I was called to return the love that the Spirit of this Place had so generously shared with us over the years—for when we excitedly walked into our special place, my heart stopped . . . and was left dangling in my breath. A violent storm had gone through. Limbs and downed trees were scattered around the site and, most painfully, two large beautiful trees lay uprooted and still across the waters of our sacred pond.

Yes, this is the wilderness. Still, my heart broke for the Spirit of this Place. As I sat at the water's edge, I thought about how our Great Mother is simply reflecting back to us through fires, droughts, and floods, tornadoes, storms, and hurricanes our long disregard for her, our pervasive inability to live as if every stone, tree, and animal is our kin in this sacred web of life—and our seemingly innate failure to recognize that when any part of this web, tenderly cradling the Soul of the World, is torn . . . we all bleed. Yes, certainly, it is tragic and devastating when large portions of our human family are impacted, but if we are all truly connected in the great web, are all a part of the Soul of the World as the ancient ones have told us, in the end, can any part be regarded as more important to the whole than another?

So, I asked myself, "What can I do, here, today?" And I instantly remembered that harmony can only be restored through reciprocity—a willingness to engage in the great dance of give and take with all of life. For so long, this special place had filled, healed, and enlivened my soul. Now it was my turn . . . to give back, to merge with the Spirit of this Place to help restore it through the offer of my love—devotional love not contingent upon weather conditions or circumstance, a love so wide, so still, so infinite it can touch the sand, stones, rocks; the marsh grasses, plants, trees; the ants, fish, birds and speak to them in *their* language. A love that permeates yet lives outside the confines of time and space, and yet is more real, more eternally present in each moment than we could ever fathom—yes, a love fully capable of making our arm bleed if we cut a tree, as Alice Walker describes in *The Color Purple*.

And so I sat quietly at the edge of the pond and sent my prayers on the windy breath of the Great Spirit into the Spirit of this Place. I called to the Spirit of the Turtle, who had long been the guardian of these waters, but he did not emerge. I thanked him for his long service over the years and sent prayers he might be well. I thanked the Spirit of the two large downed trees for having kept watch over the pond for so many years. I thanked the Spirit of the Water for providing a resting place for the trees, whose Spirits could now seek new forms over time. I imagined my love as a sacred stone dropping into the center of the pond sending out a soothing balm and, soon, I heard myself singing . . . a kind of lullaby coming from the Great Mother . . . as my body gently rocked and my soul merged with the Spirit of this Place.

I sat for a long time and was slowly aware, beyond my sadness, of a deeper, more tender love emerging than I'd ever known for this place. For now, we were silent together in the fullness of love's reciprocity where there is no beginning or end. And some sense of completeness filled my soul.

"Thank you for this blessed opportunity to serve you, to love you, as you have so loved us and given to us all these years."

And as we walked out, my heart felt light as it continued to be sung . . . and I could hear the song of the stones, trees and dragonflies echoing back in reply . . . and, together, our song filled the Soul of the World.

And I was glad.

13

Straight Up!

3 Feathers

Keep climbing . . .

leave all behind not essential to my . . .

worn floors . . . sloping now but sturdy
old cookstove . . . waiting to be fired up for chili and cornbread
screened porch . . . opening to the wild wonder
tree steps to the loft . . . holding firm as you climb
stone fireplace mantel . . . guarding all those treasures from the children

Come and rest awhile . . . and discover . . .

early morning mist holding the sunlight
daytime putter singing to the trees and darting squirrels
nighttime magic lighting the kerosine lamps and candles

Keep climbing . . .

There's a reason I'm called *heaven* you know . . .

As I tell in *A Power-Love Song*, I found my song here at 3 Feathers. It's also the place that continues to open me to the Soul of the World: to hear the trees speak, to feel the knotted, slopping, mountain teach my feet to commune with the earth, to not know where my song ends and the song of this place begins when the sound of the chattering woodpecker echoes through the sky.

"You Do Realize?!"

We didn't know it was going to happen—at least not so fast. But of course the timing was perfect. We'd sold our home of many years and had downsized into a small mill building apartment. But being the wilderness people we are, Doug immediately started looking for a camp, one we hoped would be within a reasonable driving distance so we could visit often. As most camps very close to populated areas tend to be pricey and Doug was retiring, we really didn't have a clue how we were going to make it happen. Then, of course, unexpectedly, a series of events merged in that heart-pulsing dance of divine synchronicity and . . . heaven had arrived -*again*—only this time it had a purple outhouse! I mean, really! How *could* it get any better?!

Our wonderful realtor, who'd helped us to sell our home, was a bit shocked when we called about it all excited.

"You *do* realize it has *no* plumbing, *no* electricity, *no* running water?"

"Yes!" Didn't budge the needle on our heart meter. We'd seen the pictures. This was our place!

"Uh, I think there's a hose that comes down from the underground stream up the mountain. But that's all the water that goes to the place."

"Perfect!"

"And, it's quite a long drive up."

Why *was* she discouraging us???

When we arrived to see the place, she wasn't able to make it up the drive either by car or foot, so she missed the showing. So boy, was she surprised when we called on the way home to say, "We'd like to make an offer!"

"Okay . . ." she said, slowly trying to hide that "what *are* you doing?" in her voice.

And then, all our kids thought we should seriously be committed.

"You crazy kids!"

"Are you sure you're ready for outhouse living?"

"Have you really thought this through? It looks like a lot to take on."

"Are you sure you can handle it all?"

And on and on and on!

Ahhhhhhh . . . but in just a few weeks of owning it, I'd already come to discover some important things: how much soot and ash can come out of an old antique cook stove and how good it can feel to bring it back to life; how our blessed spring bubbles up our water and sends it down the mountain straight into our sink for at least a part of the summer; how the Spirit of the Land is wild and has clearly been well-loved; how the tall trees and hovering mountains shelter us and whisper in the sweet night sounds; how the outhouse is really a step up from the in-the-dirt wilderness camping; how the old stone fireplace keeps close the special rocks from the children in days past; how a screen porch opening to the wild can be all that's needed to heal and restore a weary soul; how dirty feet, clean hands and a grateful heart are *the* most appropriate attire to dine with the Great Spirit; and, how I can walk around the land and, suddenly, without notice, irrupt into singing . . .

So, crazy? "YES!" Thank God! But it gets even better! Early on I felt like our new heaven needed a name—something that would clearly mark it as our own. I began praying for the name, for like the camp and us as the new caretakers had so effortlessly been brought together, I just knew its name was already alive in the mind of the Great Spirit.

About that time, Doug and I had gone for a walk in a park close to where we lived in town and I'd come upon three feathers. I was thrilled, as in the Native American tradition, feathers are considered special omens, a message from the Great Spirit. A few days later, as Doug and I were heading out to try a new trail near our camp, I heard myself say, "Hey, how about we call our camp 3 Feathers? Doug agreed that would be fine but pointed out I hadn't found the feathers on our land or anywhere near our mountain. So, as we started our hike, I let the idea rest.

Then, as we were heading back, I saw a beautiful large feather and then shortly after another one that looked a lot like it but was much smaller. Smiling, Doug said, "Okay, find another one and we'll call it 3 Feathers!"

Then, at the end of our hike, within feet of the Jeep, I looked off to my right over a pretty field and there it was about twenty feet out—the third feather! So now our camp had a name and over the summer Doug created a beautiful sign for our gate to add his special touch to our new name for this piece of heaven.

We often recognize divine synchronicity, the language of God, best in hindsight. It awakens us to the wonder of life and the remembrance that all that's required is we do our part. That, in fact, the Great Spirit has totally got this—us—life. It puts a giggle in our hearts and a bounce in our feet . . .

And a feather on our path.

To Love Enough

Only a few weeks after we'd bought 3 Feathers, I noticed three trees were daring to block my view of those sloping mountains off the horizon as soon as their leaves came in. *Yes,* I thought, *they'll have to go.* It was early May, and those mountains were still in full view of my dancing heart.

I was already imaging how it would be: yes, of course, I'd create a special ritual and ask permission to take them down. But, I surmised, there'd be no problem with their agreement, as I'd promise to use them as firewood. Yes, neatly glossing over the permission part, it was all quite settled—at least in my mind.

Little did I know the trees were smiling.

Indeed, over the summer months, something happened. The first time was in my hammock looking up at that wondrous tree, the one holding up the foot of my hammock. It was a bright glorious day, and I was belting out some song and remembering how George Washington Carver, mentioned in *Unripe Fruit*, had said he was able to talk with the flower, peanut, and sweet potato. It was all about love, he'd reflected. All things will give up their secrets, if you *love them enough.*

So, *why not?* I thought. Feeling like I couldn't love that tree any more, I closed my eyes, gathered in all the love, and silently asked the tree if it might share with me. Soon, I found myself gently taken inside. During my visit, the Spirit of the Tree showed me how to enter into the Soul of the World, the spirit side of things, right here in this wondrous creation of the most Holy. It reminded me that it's devotional love, empty of all desire, full and complete unto itself, that opens the mysteries of nature, as it is this love that weaves all things together in the great tapestry of life.

When it was time to leave, I thanked the Spirit of the Tree and returned to my waking state in my hammock. And I was left with a profound knowing of my oneness with all things, held and supported by the Great Spirit of Love.

One day in late August, looking out from our porch at the top of those sloping mountains on the horizon, I gasped in horror as my eyes fell on those three trees, the ones I'd marked for cutting. *Oh . . . please forgive me. I love you so. Thank you for being here and for providing a beautiful window through which those sloping mountains are made even more wondrous.*

Yes, I'd always known I was one with all in a way that lived just beyond my imagination. But now, I *knew,* ever more deeply, because . . .

a tree had taught me *to love enough.*

Asking Permission

Sometimes it's the smallest things that answer the biggest questions. Maybe that's why, even when they're right in front of us, they can often be overlooked, seem too simplistic, even frivolous. Such a time happened recently on wilderness walks with two of my grandkids—something we hadn't been able to do during the pandemic.

"Grandma! Let's go look for treasures!" my five-year-old grandson said, the one you met in *Guru "One Sock."* And with his special treasure bag close in hand, down the slope of our wilderness camp we went.

"Look at all these acorns, Grandma! Can we put them on the mantel?" As with past owners, the fireplace mantel had become our designated place for all those special treasures found on the land.

"Of course," I answered and then bent down to whisper softly in his ear, "But, did you remember to ask permission?"

His wide bright eyes shot up at me, and with a voice filled with such sweet tenderness, full of expectation, he looked down at those acorns, waiting still and silent in this small hand, and said, "Do you want to come with us acorns? Do you want to be on the mantel?" And in less than half a second, "Yes! Grandma! They said 'yes!'"

And off we went again in search of the next treasure, and the next, always repeating the same ritual we'd started doing in the wonderful wilds of his own backyard. And soon, he was struggling to haul his small bag filled with all those treasures.

A little later, my eight-year-old granddaughter, the one you met in *A Kiddy Bowl and A Grownup Spoon,* and I were walking down our steep winding driveway. We strolled slowly as she chatted about this and that.

Then, suddenly, "Look at all these pinecones, Grandma! Can we bring some to the mantel?"

"Should we ask permission?"

My granddaughter, now a little older and wiser to the ritual, said with much assurance, "Grandma! I've already asked all the pinecones around this whole place, and they've all already said 'yes!'"

"How wonderful," I said smiling, and on we went. And, then suddenly . . .

"Look Grandma! There's a big heart rock!" I strained to see it, but sure enough, off to the side, partially hidden under leaves and moss, was a large, well, somewhat heart-shaped rock waiting for one with the eyes to see.

"Let's sit, Grandma! It's too big for the mantel." And then she added quite matter-of-factly, "But don't worry, we can still sit here. I know it's okay. I've already asked permission." And so we did.

Later I thought how Native American spirituality has told us since the beginning of time about the great web of life within which we all live. Today we are witnessing a great resurgence in these ancient teachings because, I believe, our blessed earth is crying out for us to remember our ancient roots, our innate connectedness with all of life. But I know for me, imagining what I may be able to do to address our current climate-earth crisis has often felt too overwhelming to even ponder. But then an answer came on those walks—something so small, simple, playful, childlike that it was almost overlooked. I could simply say, "Did you remember to ask permission?"

Pause. Remember. Imagine how it might shift our relationship with our Great Mother Earth if we were to suddenly see, hear, taste, touch, smell every living thing as alive, worthy of our respect, worthy of our asking permission. Imagine what *we* could learn from each acorn, pinecone, rock. What if we could suddenly sense the Great Spirit growing the tree, cooing the mourning dove, budding the dandelion, stirring the waters, raising the fire? What if we could hear the voice of the wind whispering important messages to our hearts? What if we could see that everything around us is a treasure worthy of a place on the mantel?

Perhaps, just perhaps, one day, long after I am gone, one of my dear grandchildren, grown and walking with their own children or grandchildren, might say, "Let's go look for treasures! But, let's remember to ask permission to see if they want to come with us."

If so, I'll know I've done one thing well—perhaps the most important thing. I'll have helped my dear grandchildren to remember they are a part of all that is—that everything is a treasure if we have the eyes to see—everything can teach us if we have the ears to hear—and that we are each a glorious, unique and necessary part of the great web of life woven most graciously by the Great Spirit . . .

And, if so, I know I will have lived well.

PART VII

Full Circle

14

Many Are the Ways

Interfaith Ministry

On my altar, they live well together
Rosary
Traditional Mala
Mala with a Cross
Orthodox Prayer Rope
Misbaha
&
Hanging from a thick black string
An Eagle head carved from the tip of a Deer antler

Each takes me to a different scent, sight, sound of You
Yet all leave me in the same place
Silent and smiling
With nothing but Your whisper
Soft in some distant chamber of my heart

I close my eyes and see the young girl standing in my grandparents' bedroom, sucker punched, all those years ago. I hold the memory of her close with a tender smile. She couldn't have known what lay ahead, how the punch was the essential beginning, causing the stutter that would bring her to the edge of that terrifying abyss . . . to step off . . . and land in the soft hand of God. And how that would change everything.

She couldn't have known all the ways the unseen hand of God would guide her to see, hear, feel, sense, know him everywhere: by early on branding her and freeing her to have the life waiting, lifting her to fly with an eagle, startling her with his voice, healing her deepest wounds, opening her family's hidden secrets, turning her bare feet in ecstasy, kissing her in the sweet silence, peering at her from beyond the veil, showering her with abundance, sending her a blessing from Medjugorje, seeing her through the eyes of the forgotten, playing with her through the little ones, baptizing her in the sacred waters of the wilderness, and communing with her in the Soul of the World. Mostly, she'd have never believed, in the twilight years of her life, she'd be blessed to do something beautiful for him, to give back, to share with others what she'd received. She couldn't know.

You're a What?

Recall in the *Introduction: When the Katydids Went Silent*, the early stirrings of the interfaith vision seed had been planted when I was a young teen. At the front of our First Church of Religious Science sanctuary hung a large, round, stained class with symbols of the major faith traditions. I was constantly reminded to contemplate the One illuminating them all.

Twice a year, I'd go to church camps where at breakfast there'd be, for example, a place holder with a saying from the Buddha, at lunch a saying from Christ, at dinner one from Muhammad, and so on. From my earliest years, I could see, feel, believe and know I was one with all peoples everywhere. It had been awakened in my DNA but would take a lifetime to come to fruition.

By the early 2000s, seminary was calling. I knew well to whom I belonged and who it was I loved most. I'd been taking in the spiritual practices from across faith traditions for some time and had wondrously discovered God in the sweet silences, again and again. But this posed a problem. How could I possibly choose one faith over the others? Even though I'd been strongly influenced by Religious Science, I also felt a deep homegrown resonance with Christianity due to my early experiences in the small country Methodist Church. And I'd found God emanating from the practices of many other faith traditions. I knew now God could not be contained by any one of them. That religions really had little to do with God. They could offer the divinely inspired founders and events, teachings and practices, and provide a place for like-minded seekers to gather, but in the end, they could only point to God, to the mystery.

So, how elated I was the day I discovered Interfaith ministry! Now, I didn't have to choose. The program was offered by The New Seminary in New York City and, at the time, was the only inter-faith seminary in the country. It'd been founded in 1979 by a rabbi, a Catholic priest working in church reform, a former Methodist minister, and a well-known yogi swami. Yes! How often I've imagined being there to witness the historic founding, as there was no doubt *this* was where I belonged.

Looking over the two-year curriculum, I saw the second year required the creation of a minister's manual. *Wonderful!* I thought. *Maybe now I'll be able to distill, from all I've experienced, what my unique sacred path and purpose is.* Well, the second-year manual was a great assignment, asking us to research and compile samples of worship services, weddings, memorial services, grave site ceremonies, and baby blessings, but it didn't ask us to do what I was longing for. I remember thinking, *okay, maybe one day I'll create a seminary that does that.* It was a kind of prophetic moment, a foretelling of events to come.

After my ordination, I started offering worship services once a month and made myself available for other duties of ministry. And I started creating a variety of sacred studies courses for my community, sharing all I had learned and was learning, diving deep into those spiritual practices across faith traditions.

But I also noticed something else. When I'd excitedly say I'd just been ordained an Interfaith minister, the usual response was, "Wonderful!" but oftentimes, it wouldn't end there. *That* look would appear and then, "So . . . what's that? Are you Christian?" I decided I needed a way to clarify just what it was I'd become. I struggled with a number of elevator speeches. None felt adequate. Then one day I landed on a simple sentence that captured the essence: *Many are the ways we pray to one God.* The goal is unity across faith traditions, not uniformity to one. Interfaith ministry seeks to distill the One divine essence emanating from all faith traditions, ancient sacred texts, and from the face of our neighbor.

Blessedly, Interfaith ministry doesn't follow any outer religious tradition or form. Rather, it leads us to an inner campus, pointing to the exploration of our own unique expression of ministry. Some have called this our true or divine purpose. It asks that we answer the call from the One God, however we may conceive or understand this most Holy, to sound our own note in service to a greater good. It celebrates that we each have a unique part to play in the divine plan. But there is a catch. The good news is no one is going to tell you what your ministry should look like. And the bad news is no one is going to tell you what your ministry should look like!

During this time, a poem flowed from my heart, a kind of vision seed, for what was to come. It was called *What If?*

What If?
What if there was a place where we could *practice*
respecting religious differences while honoring sameness?
Perhaps then we could . . .
recognize the face of our brother and sister
beyond color, dress or language.
What if there was a place where we could *practice*
celebrating each person's unique expression of the Divine
while honoring our common heartbeat?

Perhaps then we could . . .
understand that each of us has a role to play ~ a gift to offer.
What if **there was a place where we could** practice
engaging the difficult issues while
together forging new Pathways to peace?
Perhaps then we could . . .
begin to build a world family and learn to love our neighbor as
our self.

Another prophetic moment.

Do It Now!

In 2007, immersed in the sweet silence of my spiritual practice, I heard a clear directive to start a yearlong study and to call it "Living Our Purpose: The Heart of Spiritual Practice." *What???* Such a thing was nowhere on my radar. It was early fall, and other classes were underway. I was very busy. And in addition, I was clearly directed to get on the phone and call all those I thought might be interested. Now, I was *not* happy about this, as this was definitely *not* my style. This is why I often say my assignments come *through* me—not *from* me. But by that time, I certainly knew it'd be futile to resist.

So I got on the phone, and by the end of the day I had enough people to fill two classes! Now, mind you, neither I nor they had any idea what I was going to teach. But this is how it starts. Trust. I ran the course for two years and, as it turned out, the handouts I created for the classes became the first draft of the curriculum for the seminary I'd soon be told to start. I love God!

And so it was in the fall of 2009, immersed again in sweet silence, I heard the directive to start the seminary program *and* to call it "The Path of Crow: Discover Your Direct Path to God." And again, *What???* I hadn't been a minister very long and definitely didn't feel ready to start a seminary. But what I did know was that I wanted to give others the opportunity to experience what I had—to know that, truly, *many are the ways we pray to one God*—through the immersion in spiritual practices across faith traditions. I wanted them to fully *know* this from their own experience, not just believe it.

Holding this intention close, I put out a short email asking for a few people to help me start an Interfaith seminary program based on spiritual practice. There was an overwhelming response. And so we began, using the first draft of those handouts I'd created as the curriculum, and the Tree of Life Interfaith Seminary was born. Later, I'd be directed to create a spiritual mentoring program as an optional third year. Finally, in June of 2010, it was time for the Tree of Life Interfaith Temple, a 501c3, to be formed to rightly serve as the ordinating body for the first seminary class of 2011, and for all classes to follow. Now the "What If?" vision seed was beginning to blossom.

Over the coming years, I was blessed to train and ordain participants in eight seminary classes and five spiritual mentoring classes and lead our church as Presiding Minister. Then in 2018, I made the decision to step down to give some of my ordained ministers a chance to lead and offer new ways to bring forth our amazing, and much-needed, vision. In addition, both the seminary and spiritual mentoring programs were redesigned to accommodate many more potential students, far more than I could alone.

I've always said I wanted our Tree of Life Interfaith Temple and Seminary to begin with me, not end with me. I'd been given the vision seed to plant and the great honor to nurture it for a while. Now it was time for it to grow to new heights under the care of others. Today, I graciously continue to serve as Founding Minister and spiritual advisor.

Pray. Sit in silence. Listen. God will do the rest. After all, in the end, it's not about *us*. We're just here to serve a purpose, to sound our note in the divine chorus. And sometimes, if we're lucky, just quiet enough, we can hear the angels sing and know that we, too, are a glorious, humble, part of God's love song for all creation.

And, in such moments, we can only bow in gratitude as our bare feet dance with gladness.

15

Lifted Up

Grace Beyond Measure and the Final Test

And as dusk soothes and gathers me in
my feet . . . too busy to notice . . .
kept kissing the ground
singing a love song
for You.

And God said, "Come. There's a blessing for you so you may know the true fullness of My grace, and a final test so I may claim you as My own."

The Picture in My Pocket

I'd tucked a small picture of her in the pocket of my dress, the one I wore under the commencement robe on graduation day. For a long time I'd known she'd have to be there, close. I wanted her to see, hear, and feel it all, for, in every way, this day was for her.

It wasn't my plan to go back to school for a doctorate in my mid-sixties. I'd actually only made the initial inquiry to squelch the relentless encouragement to do so from my friend Betty who, at the time, was in the doctoral program at Andover Newton Theological School. She felt I needed the degree to bring credentials to my books and to support the expansion of my work to a larger audience. I wasn't convinced. After all, I'd done pretty well without a doctorate. I'd self-published several books, created an interfaith seminary, and had founded a church. But shortly after the initial inquiry, divine synchronicity kicked in, and sure enough, I was accepted into the doctoral program.

However, once the excitement of being accepted faded, old inner doubts began to surface, the ones still held by that young girl of long ago. *What are you doing? Are you crazy?* she'd protest in vulnerable moments. And, while I'd try to remind her that we'd gone to graduate school and had actually done quite well, it didn't matter. She continued to complain. *That was a special situation. This is different—a traditional school. We didn't do so well back then!*

So, on the day of my graduation, I knew that young girl had to be with me. I was graduating with honors and had been inducted into the Jonathon Edwards Society. I wanted her to be there so she could know, *See, you were always smart and fully capable. I know you didn't believe it. But you always were.*

I sat in the third row next to my friend Holly. As the speeches wore on, I found myself wandering back to moments I knew she'd remember . . . moments like being told in my senior year of high school by a teacher who had a very caring way, "You know, dear, college isn't for everyone." But I'd be accepted into the University of Southern Mississippi largely because my mother was an alum. Later, when graduating from college with that low GPA and GRE score, my advisor would say much the same, adding, "You know, graduate school does require a certain level of aptitude." Also said in a caring way, she was trying to prepare me for the inevitable rejections she knew would come if I were to pursue graduate school.

But mostly, my heart wandered back to that day in my sophomore year of high school when Miss Shirley Curtis said she was going to recommend me for speech tournaments because she'd said, "You have something to say." Oh my, dear one, do you remember when Dr. Drummond wrote to us, "Your work on the spirituality of sound is going to be groundbreaking, mark my words." Do you remember? Yes, even here, in this traditional environment, you certainly did have something to say.

And about that time, I was abruptly jolted back . . .

"And the Frederick Buechner Award for Excellence in Writing on the Doctor of Ministry level is awarded to . . ." Stunned, I didn't get up right away until Holly poked me.

"Congratulations!"

So, together, I and the picture of me in my pocket as that young girl walked up onto the stage in front of a full auditorium to receive our award. I know for her it must have all seemed like such a dream. It was for me too.

And the grace wouldn't stop flowing. My dissertation, "The Call of the Mourning Dove: How Sacred Sound Awakens Mystical Unity," was accepted for publication by a well-respected academic publisher, and my nationally recognized theology professor, Dr. S. Mark Heim, contributed the foreword. And later, the new paradigm I'd proposed, the Sonic Trilogy of Love, would become a foundational theological blueprint, as simply the Trilogy of Love, for my church. Now, in spite of a lifetime of unforeseen mystery, wonder and beauty, if you'd told me and that young girl all of this at the start of the doctoral program, well, we still would've surely thought you were crazy.

Oh, the things we hear and then carry for a lifetime, things we fully and completely believe, without question, and yet *are not true at all*. Such is the power of those early messages. How they stay with us until, maybe, one day we're given the chance to prove them wrong.

I offer this story to all our young ones inside, for we all have them, whether we've acknowledged them or not. They carry those old messages, hardened into core beliefs, and can lie dormant for a lifetime, just below the surface, dogging us sometimes, with not-so-subtle nips at our heels. But the truth is we can never move fast enough to shake them because they *are* us, those most-tender-tucked-away parts, which, in the end, are just chasing after our acceptance and love.

And so, it'd been on the morning of *our* graduation day, all dressed up and ready to go, that I'd paused and stared softly into those eyes looking back at me from the old picture. I pressed it tight against my chest as the tears came—tears from my heart's deepest underground spring, welling up now and gushing out, releasing a flood of joyful gratitude. Then, I'd snuggled the picture back into my pocket.

"Let's go, Stephanie," I'd said, smiling. "This is your special day."

And so it was.

Onto the Stage!

"You and I have the power to change the world—one encounter at a time," I declared with a heart explosion, looking out over the auditorium and into the cameras. This was how I started my TEDx talk, but I didn't know I was going start that way until that morning—yes, that very morning—not until after the early arrival, after we nine speakers had gathered briefly to prepare ourselves for the day, not until our host for the event, who happened to be my speaker coach, was giving us a pep talk and said without much fanfare, "Each of you has the power to change the world with your talk."

In that *awe*-mazing instant, I felt a familiar jolt and knew, clearly, I'd just been given instructions to reframe my entire talk with this inspirational glue. I decided to start with "You and I" to emphasize inclusion and to add "one encounter at a time" to frame my talk's three stories. Later, my coach would tell me he was thinking of my talk when he made that statement. How wondrously God's unseen hand works!

Now until then, I'd been very happy with my talk but couldn't say I was on fire with it. I'd chalked it up to being exceptionally busy in other areas of my life and had decided to simply trust that in *the* moment the Holy Spirit would come through, as had long been my experience. After all, I did fully believe in the message— it *was* possible, indeed critical to our very survival, for each of us to reach across political, religious, and socioeconomic divides to connect with those whom we viewed as *the other* or very different from us. It *was* possible, if we could only allow ourselves to catch a glimpse of our common humanity, that's *what's the same in all of us*. And I felt by sharing true personal stories that had informed me, I could authentically demonstrate the possibility.

I could end my reporting of the day's events here, for I feel very blessed to say the talk couldn't have gone better. But in truth, a greater story had been unfolding over the six months leading up to the talk. A story that speaks to how, if we're to serve a greater good, as I believed my talk was inspired to do, we must prepare ourselves for what is being asked.

This often puts us on what Joseph Campbell described as a monomyth, or a hero-heroine's journey. Here, the heroine goes on a journey, faces some decisive crisis, and, if victorious, comes home changed. The critical aspect of the journey is to transform the fears and roadblocks that stand in the way of a victorious ascent, or expansion, into the next level of consciousness being required by the task at hand. How romantic it all sounds on paper. How absolutely terrifying, beyond all measure, in real life.

It'd all started innocently enough. The subject line in the October 2017 email read simply, "One More Thing." It was from my friend Christy, who wrote, "You may be getting something in the mail from TEDx. I hope it's OK but I nominated you to be one of the speakers at their next event in June 2018." *What?!!* Sure enough, I received information and was invited to apply, along with over eighty others, for one of the nine spots. Next, I was interviewed, and in December learned I'd been chosen. Until that point, I was totally excited about it, completely focused on winning one of those prize spots.

But soon after the initial excitement began to settle, the impact of what had happened and what it could mean started overshadowing all anticipation. Now, fully committed to giving the TEDx talk, my young girl inside started freaking out! Yes, she knew now she was smart, but to get up on a stage in front of hundreds of people and then to know the talk would be on YouTube . . . well, *that* was entirely different! Some mornings I'd wake up with such dread I could hardly get out of bed. I've often imagined it was something like Arjuna must have felt in the Bhagavad Gita. Clearly called to do his duty on the battlefield of life in service to a greater good, he found himself suddenly feeling wimpy, cowardly, and resisting vehemently. And so did I.

So early on, I started praying with the most tender, deep yearning I'd ever known that I would enjoy the connection with the One who'd always spoken for me when I could not—especially now when I was feeling most afraid. One day, blessedly, Mother Mary came to me and gave me a beautiful vision to sustain me throughout the coming months. It was an image of me as that young girl standing at her side, and of her taking my hand and leading me out onto the stage. There, I morphed into my grown self and was shown what was to come and most lovingly assured all would be well.

I knew clearly this would be the second time Mother Mary had come to save me. Every night, I slept with my Mother Teresa rosary close by, and part of my daily prayers became the beautiful hymn "You Raise Me Up." All along I held fast to the vision I'd been given but found my young girl inside still needed reassurance that she could indeed rise up to meet the challenge. So together we prayed constantly that the love of God would have its way with us and that the vision would be fulfilled.

And, graciously, it was.

When, being last, it was finally my turn to speak, I was waiting in the wings, praying hard and thanking Mother Mary for being with me. And then I heard, "Join me in welcoming. . ." and as I took my first step, I instantly felt a kind of wind under my feet. It was like I was literally being lifted and propelled forward—almost like I wanted to skip—yet my footsteps were grounded, solid, and focused. I felt completely calm, peaceful, present, and, most of all, laser clear about what was being asked of me. My stories rang out strong as I shared how each had catapulted me into a place of great hope that it *was* possible to find one another beyond the crippling political, religious, and socioeconomic divisiveness of the day. I could feel clearly how the message was *so* much bigger than me and that I was simply the reporter, the messenger, for with every word, love had its way that day. Love, indeed, had its way.

I've heard from many who were there.

"It was like time stood still."

"You held all of us."

"People around me were crying."

And on and on. Even now it's hard to speak of it.

Yet while some might describe this experience as a kind of monomyth or heroine's journey, to me, in the end, it didn't feel that way, for I knew *I can take absolutely no credit*. I did not create the blessed vision Mother Mary showed me. I couldn't have anticipated the words my coach would say that morning, reframing my talk. And I certainly didn't create the wind beneath my feet, propelling me forward, any more than it was I who created fluent speech in those tournaments and classrooms all those years ago.

No, rather, I've come to believe that, as it's always been, it was God making me, for the moment, like the moon, a hallowed reflection, an instrument of his grace, goodness, beauty, and truth.

And, in the aftermath, I am left silent, humble, and . . . ecstatically still in the wonder of God.

www.ingramcontent.com/pod-product-compliance
Lightning Source LLC
Chambersburg PA
CBHW062222080426
42734CB00010B/1986